HOW TO BE AN AGILE
BUSINESS ANALYST

KENT J MCDONALD

Dedication

This book is for all of those business analysts working inside organizations who are just sure there is more to working on an agile team than standing up and writing user stories.

TABLE OF CONTENTS

FOREWORD

I landed my first project as an agile business analyst back in 2008. Interestingly enough, I was hired for my experience analyzing requirements in use cases. Midway through the project, the organization decided to outsource the software development to a team that was using agile practices. This very traditional role quickly became an agile one.

Unlike many business analysts facing agile transitions, my role was never threatened. Everyone was painfully aware that they needed a business analyst to bridge the gaps between the myriad business stakeholders with knowledge of different aspects of the business and the software development team.

Even so, my world was pretty much turned upside down.

By this point in my career, even though I wasn't officially an agile business analyst, I wasn't exactly a traditional one either.

- I had long given up 50-page specifications in favor of a short scope statement and a list of key features.
- I leveraged short textual and visual models, primarily use cases and wireframes, to quickly gain buy-in and communicate about the requirements with both business and technical stakeholders.
- I valued communication, collaboration, and decision making over documentation.

However, being asked to give up my beloved use cases in favor of user stories and my use case list for a product backlog made me feel like I had no idea what I was doing. I felt conceptually stuck as to how to move forward.

I actually waited for my copy of *User Stories Applied* by Mike Cohn to show up in the mail before I dug in and got to work. Like so many of the business analysts I train today, writing user stories became my perception of what an agile business analyst was.

After eight two-week sprints, we delivered an operational and extremely successful piece of software. More importantly, we addressed a real business problem by eliminating a lot of back and forth paperwork for the business.

And, perhaps for the first time in my career, I felt like I knew exactly what was going to be delivered, and that I was able to communicate about what was most important about the project and why, and that I could help the business stakeholders make informed decisions about what to prioritize when we started reaching the limit of our schedule and budget.

This new level of awareness got me hooked on agile practices, because I saw how they worked. I experienced firsthand how they helped me be more effective at ensuring real business problems were solved, and that our development budget was leveraged effectively.

I also learned something that has stuck with me ever since: There is a lot more to the work I do as a business analyst than the type of documentation I create or how my requirements are organized.

Today, I still stand in my truth that on every successful project you'll find a business analyst. They may not have the title, but someone is helping drive alignment and clarity and is focused on the positive change the project creates for an organization.

And that person is a business analyst. (Even if they don't have the title or, more commonly, the awareness that they are indeed a business analyst.)

However, I think the fears we face as business analysts in an increasingly agile world are real, and to a certain extent, well founded.

I don't believe that our profession is becoming irrelevant—business analysis is more important than ever to make sure we leverage our resources to solve problems that really need solving—but I do see agile trends as a real wake-up call.

A wake-up call that, as business analysts:

- We absolutely cannot organize our work and our thinking solely around documentation;
- More documentation is not better and not a sign of a job well, or completely, done; and
- We cannot hold tight to our ivory towers or specific practices and expect to remain relevant.
- But also, a wake-up call that it's our time:
- To lead the path to increased efficiency, to focus more on communication and analysis and ensuring that the requirements (however we organize them) solve real business problems;
- To be more agile and cultivate our agility mindset, even if we're in a traditional organization; and
- To see agile transformations as opportunities to improve business analysis practices, rather than step back in fear and scramble around trying to learn how to write user stories.

Our current business environment provides tremendous opportunities for professionals who desire to create and inspire positive change. Agile trends allow us to redefine our roles, practices, and communication techniques in ways that deliver more value, cut out a lot of unnecessary documentation work, and make our jobs even more rewarding.

Because I love this profession with all my heart and being, I say "YES, PLEASE!"

And we need leaders like Kent McDonald to pull us through this. Leaders who are truly business analysts, who value the skills we bring to the table as business analysts, and who have deep experience on agile teams and leading agile transformations.

Kent has given us a real gift with this book. Instead of following my path and scrambling to learn how to write user stories (and falsely assuming you have to throw all your business analysis practices out the window on your first agile project), you can learn from Kent how to really, truly be an agile business analyst.

Along the way, Kent clears up misunderstandings about both agile and business analysis, and dispels myths about how these practices intersect to create positive change for our organizations. He teaches you how to apply your business analysis skills in an agile manner, so you can step up and be a part of the change instead of retreating in fear of that change.

He gives you the gift of confidence by showing you the path to working effectively on a team working in an agile fashion. And he will help you demonstrate why other teams in your organization should include you. Because even though we know that on every successful project you'll find a business analyst, there are still misconceptions out there and it's our job to address them.

We've heard the wake-up call. Let's do something about it.

My call to you is to take something in this book and apply it in your work this week. How can you bring the agile mindset to your work as a business analyst? How will this make you even more valuable, more relevant, and more effective in your role?

"Be the change you wish to see in the world." The time to start is now.

Laura Brandenburg, CBAP
Founder and Creator, Bridging the Gap
http://www.bridging-the-gap.com[1]

---

[1] http://www.bridging-the-gap.com/

CHAPTER 1 – INTRODUCTION

There are two cornerstone ideas in this book.

First, agile is an adjective. It's not a *thing* or a *methodology*, it's a way you can approach knowledge work.

Second, your team can benefit from business analysis even if they're working in an agile manner.

Accordingly, this book is about applying your business analysis skills in an agile manner. You'll still see the term agile business analyst, but agile as it is used in this book describes how you approach business analysis, not a specific role or job title.

This book attempts to clear up misunderstandings and dispel myths around the intersection (or lack thereof) of business analysis and agile. You still need business analysis when working in an agile fashion.

This explores how you can help your team understand the applicable business rules and processes and to make sure you're building the right thing.

This book will help make you confident about being a product member of a team working in an agile manner.

So, while it won't help you argue for having a business analyst role on a team, it will help you demonstrate to teams in your organization why they should have *you* on their team.

Who this book is for

If you are currently in a business analyst job, are filling a business analyst role, or have a significant business analysis background and want to learn more about agile, this book is for you.

You may be working at an organization that is starting an agile transformation you've been asking for and may even be driving to make happen.

You may be having agile "done to you" at your current organization, and figure you may as well understand what this agile thing is and whether it's worth trying to play along.

You may be looking for a different opportunity and find that every interesting job opportunity you see is looking for an "agile business analyst" or says their organization does agile.

Or you may work at an organization that has been working in an agile manner for a while, and you just want to improve your team's effectiveness by applying those business analysis skills you've practiced for years.

In all those situations and others, this book will help.

I point out the not quite ideal solutions (having agile done to you, for example) because I feel it's important to portray things the way they really are. There are organizations that have adopted an agile way of working and are reaping the benefits. There are also organizations that have gone through multiple failed agile transformations and keep coming back for more. Other organizations are somewhere in the middle, existing in some agile purgatory where they partake in agile theater but never grasped how to get the true benefits of an agile mindset. This book helps in all of those situations because it focuses on what you can do to be effective, not on the right or wrong way to make an organization "agile."

What context this book applies to

Most business analysts interested in agile are working for an organization that builds or maintains software for internal use or are going through some form of digital transformation.

They work for organizations that do not sell software as their actual product but use software to support their business activities or enable the sale and support of their actual product or service. I generally refer to that sort of software as *internal products*. You work on internal products if you:

- Work in an IT organization that builds its own software for use inside the organization.
- Purchase commercial off-the-shelf (COTS) software and then configure it and integrate it with other products. (You probably also customize the software, but that's not something I generally recommend.)
- Use Software as a Service (SaaS) to support business operations.
- Work on your organization's website or mobile apps.
- Work on software that involves your customers directly in your business processes instead of having an employee in the middle.

These last two items are what people typically mean when they talk about digital transformations.

Yes, I realize that business analysts can also work on business process related activities, or be involved in business architecture. Apart from where those activities support work on an internal product, I'm not discussing those contexts in this book. That's not to imply that those contexts don't exist or are not important.

I focused on product development in the specific instances noted above because it's where I believe there's a need, it's where agile is particularly relevant, and frankly it's where my experience lies.

I would like to be able to talk about these efforts solely in terms of product development. Unfortunately, many organizations still use a project management paradigm to manage the work they do to deliver internal products, so to act like project management does not exist anymore would be irresponsible.

Throughout this book I talk about both project management and product management and have tried to be explicit about which paradigm I mean. Here's my view of each so when I refer to them, you can understand what I have in mind. Some of the specifics from this comparison are based on a presentation from Allan Kelly[2] and other work of the #noprojects[3] crowd.

My view of project management mirrors the description provided by the Project Management Institute:[4] a temporary endeavor undertaken to create a unique product, service, or result.

Project management is generally based on a set of assumptions that, while they hold true for many types of endeavors, generally aren't valid for the type of systems and applications that can be thought of as internal products.

Project management is concerned with delivering a solution. Product management is concerned with determining whether a solution is needed and what that solution should look like.

Project management measures success based on staying within time, cost, and scope (output) constraints. Product management measures success based on outcome.

Projects are temporary. Software products (the successful ones at least) continue to change as your users' needs change or as you get a more refined understanding of those needs.

Projects are performed by temporary organizations which disband after the project is completed. That dissolution of the team destroys knowledge capability and performance. Products are maintained on an ongoing basis by the same team. Keeping a team together builds knowledge capability and performance.

---

[2] https://vimeo.com/163976496
[3] http://noprojects.org/
[4] https://www.pmi.org/about/learn-about-pmi/what-is-project-management

Projects usually grow in order to pass through typical budget processes. This results in large deliveries with considerable lead time between them. When a team can work on a continuous basis on a product, changes can be delivered in small batches, which helps to reduce risk due to rapid feedback and increase return because users have access to new capabilities sooner.

Organizations are much more familiar, and comfortable, with budgeting for work using a project paradigm. In other words, define a specific output and declare a specific budget and timeframe in which that output will be delivered, and then measure success against those plans. Even though this approach is fraught with errors, organizations prefer that familiar approach to planning over the more realistic but more uncertain product based approach.

Until organizations decide to fund teams to work on products and identify specific outcomes they would like to accomplish, project management will be a reality in most software organizations, so agile business analysts need to know how to deal with it.

Organizations generally use projects to organize work on specific products. Even "product based" organizations will fall into that pattern, often using a project to authorize a specific piece of work on a product, even if it's the same team that has worked on that product before.

It's not ideal but it is the current reality, and it's the general scheme I'll assume in this book.

How to use this book

You can read the book cover to cover, or you can read specific sections when the occasion calls for it.

If you would like more insight into my perspective on the intersection of business analysis and agile, you may want to read Chapters 2 and 3.

Chapters 4–7 describe four factors that can help you frame your context and choose appropriate practices:

- Your organization's strategy
- Your organization's structure
- Your product
- Customers, users, and stakeholders

Chapters 8 – 11 give more specifics on how you can exhibit the characteristics I apply to agile business analysts.

Chapter 12 explores Bridging the Gap's eight-step business analysis process[5] from an agile perspective.

One tough thing about writing a book is deciding what to include and what to leave out to make it readily accessible. As I put this book together, there were many things that I couldn't keep, so I've provided links to further information throughout the book. If you're reading this electronically those links will be in the text and will show up as footnotes. If you're reading this book the old-fashioned way (on paper) the links will only show up as footnotes.

You can also visit https://www.kbp.media/go/agile-ba-book/[6] to get a full list of the resources listed in the book.

---

5 https://www.bridging-the-gap.com/business-analysis-process/
6 https://www.kbp.media/go/agile-ba-book/

CHAPTER 2 – AGILE IS A MINDSET

Agile has reached—and blazed past—buzzword status.

It's no longer new (the term applied to software development in 2001), yet people are still learning about it for the first time. When they do, they frequently refer to agile as a software development methodology, a product development methodology, or a project management methodology.

It's none of those things, or any kind of thing. Agile is a way of looking at and thinking about how to approach knowledge work.

It's not a noun. It's an adjective.

It's not a methodology. It's a mindset.

As Alistair Cockburn described it, a methodology is the set of conventions your team agrees to follow. Scrum, Kanban, SAFe, etc. are frameworks that teams use as a starting point for creating their methodology to fit their context. (Some people in the Scrum and SAFe worlds forget that.)

What an agile mindset looks like

There have been a few attempts at describing an agile mindset.

We started with the Manifesto for Agile Software Development. The Agile Manifesto[7] began with the key sentence "We are uncovering better ways of developing software by **doing it and helping others do it**" (emphasis mine), and then proceeded to share four values and 12 principles focused on the challenges of software development teams and based on the situation in 2001.

---

[7] http://agilemanifesto.org/

Then there was the much less known document—the Declaration of Interdependence—which tried to bring leadership into the picture.

Recently we've seen several other views, including Modern Agile[8] and many others, usually in the form of some sort of manifesto.

When you have an agile mindset, you accept the fact that you face uncertainty—that you can't know everything when you start working on something. When you have an agile mindset, you approach things in a way that allows you to continuously learn and adapt. You seek to remove that uncertainty. When you have an agile mindset, your goal is to deliver a desired outcome—you satisfy your customers' needs.

Adopting an agile mindset

When people adopt agile, undergo an agile transformation, or "have agile done to them" they learn about one of several frameworks, for example, Extreme Programming (XP)[9], Scrum,[10] or SAFe.[11] They learn about techniques, artifacts, roles, and ceremonies.

Those techniques, artifacts, roles, and ceremonies are designed to help you behave in a way aligned with that mindset. But until you know **why** you do those things you won't understand the mindset.

To adopt an agile mindset, you and your team need to continuously ask yourselves these questions and behave accordingly:

- Do we understand the outcome we're trying to deliver?
- How can we understand that outcome better?

---

8 http://modernagile.org/
9 https://www.agilealliance.org/glossary/xp/
10 https://www.agilealliance.org/glossary/scrum/
11 https://www.scaledagileframework.com/

- Will this backlog item help us deliver that outcome?
- Are there things we aren't sure about?
- What can we do to learn about those things?
- Are there things we're doing that we don't need to do anymore?
- Are there things we're not doing that we should?
- How can we apply what we've learned to better satisfy our customer's needs and improve our organization's results?

Don't get hung up on what the framework says.

Don't assume that because a practice is part of a framework that you have to keep doing it even when it no longer makes sense.

Don't worry about what "agile says." (Agile doesn't say anything.) And please, don't use the reason "that's not agile." That may be a sign that you're using agile as a club rather than a tool.

Resist the urge to label what you're doing. You don't need to call it Scrum, or agile, or lean. If you need to call it anything, call it "what works here."

Labels don't matter.

What does matter is that you focus on a clear outcome and that you take steps to constantly learn. You seek to continuously understand your customers' needs better. You seek a better understanding of their desired outcome. You seek to continuously be more effective at satisfying those needs. The ceremonies, the roles, the techniques? They can be helpful if you keep in mind why you do them. Forget that, and they become agile theater.

Approach business analysis with an agile mindset

When you clearly understand the desired outcome and focus on delivering that outcome, you avoid delivering things that aren't necessary.

When you seek to continuously learn about your customers and their needs, you can define the right outcome with the minimum amount of output.

When you continuously learn the best way to work with your team, you make sure you have a shared understanding about what they need to deliver and why.

In short, you become more effective.

Your team will want to work with you on future products.

Your organization will view you as someone who gets the right things done.

There's more to agile than Scrum

Ask anyone to describe agile, and inevitably they'll use terms like sprint, product backlog, product owner, and sprint planning. Those are all terms specific to Scrum that have become, for better or worse, part of the ubiquitous language of agile.

The Scrum framework has won the market share wars and is the most commonly used framework when organizations adopt agile. That popularity leads many people to conclude that agile = Scrum.

In reality, Scrum is one of many frameworks you can use as a starting point to approach work in an agile fashion. I like to use an analogy here: *Scrum is to agile as Kleenex is to facial tissue.*

Why is that important? Because Scrum is only one way to exhibit an agile mindset, it is not appropriate in every situation, and it is not a complete solution.

If people think that they have to do Scrum in order to be agile, they conclude they have to have sprints, even when the nature of work lends itself to prioritizing and deploying much more frequently than once every two weeks. It also leads them to ignore the excellent technical practices found in XP.

The thing to remember is that while Scrum is a useful component to practicing agile, it is not sufficient by itself, and it is not required. As with all the frameworks that have sprung up around the agile community, Scrum has certain advantages and is appropriate in some situations and not so much in others.

How to choose a framework

A timeboxed approach (Scrum) may work for you if you've got a fairly significant initiative. This kind of methodology works well when you need to break work into smaller chunks to get more frequent feedback and have some intermediate feedback.

A timeboxed approach may work for you if your team needs some help focusing on a specific set of items for a short time—say, a couple of weeks.

A flow approach (such as Kanban[12]) may work for you if new work arrives frequently and unpredictably, such that you can't plan what to work on for two weeks.

A flow approach may work for you if each item of work you do is independent of every other item and it doesn't add value to delay deploying a completed item while you wait for other items to get done.

---

[12] https://www.agilealliance.org/glossary/kanban/

Good engineering practices (such as those described in XP) are always a good thing to adopt when you work in software product development.

You may find that it's helpful to combine different frameworks. For example, you may plan using timeboxes, but follow a flow approach within those timeboxes and incorporate several good engineering practices. Or, you may follow a flow approach but plan and retrospect on a regular basis.

The key is for your team to create a methodology based on the framework(s) that seem to fit your context and adapt that approach through ongoing reflection and adaptation.

To understand your context in a way that helps your team create your methodology, it's good to understand the risks you face. A variety of factors impact the framework you use as a basis for your team's methodology. Two of the key factors are the uncertainty you have about your product and the complexity involved in delivering it. The context leadership model,[13] created by Todd Little, helps your team explore the complexity and uncertainty you face, establish a methodology, and select techniques to deal with the risks that result.

Analysis is still relevant

Business analysts often interpret the lack of mention of business analysis in most agile frameworks (Scrum, XP, SAFe) to mean that there is no place for analysis, and hence no place for business analysts in an agile setting.

Everything about that interpretation is wrong.

In general, the frameworks (except perhaps for SAFe) are not intended to be all-encompassing. They are starting points from which teams can build their own methodologies. One thing that

---

[13] https://www.kbp.media/context-leadership-model/

your team will inevitably add to your methodology is some way to make sure you all understand what you are supposed to build.

The agile frameworks were created by software developers to solve problems that software developers face. Each framework includes a role that is responsible for determining the right thing for the team to work on. In Scrum it's the product owner. In XP, it's the onsite customer. Most of those frameworks do not say how that is done.

That's where analysis comes in. Elicitation, process analysis, data analysis, and other analysis techniques help your team build a shared understanding of the desired outcome and help you to determine the best solution.

These analysis techniques are not your end result. They are merely tools to help you add value to your team.

To do that:

- You do small bits of analysis throughout the entire effort to keep the team's focus on the desired outcome and build and maintain a shared understanding.
- You pass on what you have learned to the rest of the team—both the output of the analysis techniques and the techniques themselves.
- You make sure that key decisions get made. When those decisions are your responsibility, you make timely, informed decisions. When others are responsible for those decisions, you make sure they have the information they need to make timely, informed decisions.

Analysis techniques are still useful, but you'll find that how and when you use them changes. You perform small amounts of analysis more frequently to aid communication and build a shared understanding, rather than do all your analysis at once to produce the only means of communicating.

Agile alone will not get you better, faster, cheaper

> There is nothing quite so useless as doing with great efficiency something that should not be done at all.
> – Peter Drucker

Many IT organizations adopt agile in an attempt to do things better, faster, and cheaper. They are often disappointed.

Agile can help you do things better if your team adopts the engineering practices often associated with XP.

Agile can help you deliver things faster and cheaper if you take the opportunity to cut out processes you don't need and you continuously improve.

IT organizations are often disappointed because things don't get as better, faster, and cheaper as they were hoping or were led to believe.

When organizations adopt agile in their IT and development organizations and do not make corresponding changes in how they manage their portfolio of work, they soon find that they have become more efficient at producing the wrong things.

You can see benefit from improving how your team works together and how you develop, test, and deploy software. You won't see the benefits you sought until you figure out how to deliver the right thing and not deliver everything else.

The agile frameworks don't provide practical guidance on how to determine the right thing to deliver. They punt that responsibility to a role without any suggestion on how to make that happen.

You need to supplement the agile mindset and an agile framework with practices that help you understand the need you're trying to satisfy, the solution you're going to use to do that, and a way to make decisions along the way.

The set of practices you use depends a great deal on your context.

If you're customer facing use product management

If you're doing something customer facing, such as a website or mobile app, then the practices you should apply can be found in the *product* management realm.

You may not have a clear understanding of your customers' needs, or even if there is a need to satisfy. Once you identify the need you may not have a clear idea of the best solution, because your customers have a choice of whether they use your product. Product management is primarily focused on clearing away the uncertainty around customer needs and discovering appropriate solutions to address those needs that your customers will actually use.

There has been a lot of work in the product management space on interviewing and understanding customers and users, which can be helpful if you are working on something that you expect your customers to interact with directly.

If you're internal facing use portfolio management

If you're doing something internally focused such as customer relationship management (CRM), enterprise resource planning (ERP), or any other TLA (three-letter acronym) system imaginable, you probably need portfolio management.

You need to think about how things line up with your organization's strategy—which ultimately should be based on satisfying your customers' needs.

You are aware of the problem, and probably have a good idea about the solution as well, although you may not be sure how much of the solution you need to provide to address the problem, or the best way to implement that solution. You're in the Cynefin[14] complicated domain.

Portfolio management techniques provide ways to make decisions that allow you to focus. Not trying to do everything, but homing in on the important things to do right now, which things to delay, and which things to not do at all because they don't align with your organization's strategy and your customers' best interests.

Whether product or portfolio, you need to learn

Whichever way you choose, you need to incorporate learning into determining the right thing to deliver.

In customer-facing contexts, you want to learn about the need and the solution. Many product management techniques are built around understanding customers, users, and their needs.

You're also not guaranteed to know for sure if people are going to use the item, so you need to find ways to verify that your customers and users have the problem you're trying to fix and would use your solution to address it.

If you are internally focused, you want to learn how well the solution you landed upon will address the need you're trying to satisfy. Seek out the true need. Don't just take your users' request for granted and treat them explicitly as feature requests.

You need to be adaptive, but you need to get enough done to possess validated learning. That means it doesn't do you any good to shift direction midstream without a good reason.

Only when organizations combine proper decision making and a focus on outcomes with well-functioning development teams

---

[14] https://www.everydaykanban.com/2013/09/29/understanding-the-cynefin-framework/

that build quality into what they build do they truly realize the benefits of an agile mindset.

Writing and slicing user stories is not the whole story

Business analysis does not exist to elicit, document, and manage requirements. It exists to "enable change in an enterprise by defining needs and recommending solutions that deliver value to stakeholders" according to A Guide to the Business Analysis Body of Knowledge (BABOK Guide v3).[15] Requirements are only a means to those ends.

Along those same lines, there's much more to analysis with an agile mindset than writing user stories and slicing them down to a certain size. Those are just a couple of mechanisms you can use to help build a shared understanding with your team about the problem and the solution.

There are many other techniques that are helpful to have in your toolkit: job stories, specification by example, story mapping, context diagrams, process decomposition, mockups, wireframes, and a host of others.

The next time you get hung up on how you write user stories, tell yourself that stories are placeholders for a conversation. As long as you write something that reminds you what you need to talk about, that's sufficient.

You don't need to write everything using "As A, I Want, So That." No matter what you stuff into that phrase it won't fully explain what you're trying to convey. The techniques I listed above and describe later in the book will tell the story much better.

---

[15] https://www.iiba.org/standards-and-resources/babok/

Final thoughts

With the proper mindset and a great deal of self-discipline, your team can be successful with minimal process.

Without the proper mindset, teams must continuously add process to aid the collaboration that comes naturally to those who have the right mindset. I encourage you to think about how you can adopt an agile mindset, to help you achieve the right outcome for your stakeholders more effectively.

If you're looking for assistance with how to do that, keep reading!

CHAPTER 3 – WHAT IS AN AGILE BUSINESS ANALYST

You are not an agile business analyst just because you have a working knowledge of Scrum, you are able to write user stories, or you got a certification.

You are an agile business analyst when you **consider your context** so that you use appropriate techniques. You learn more about your customers and users and their needs. You learn more about the constraints that your stakeholders want to apply to your project.

You are an agile business analyst when you help your team focus on delivering **maximum outcome with minimum outputs** and use that outcome to define success and measure progress.

An outcome is the change you're trying to introduce to the world. It's why you started a project to make changes to your product. Outputs are the things you produce—like requirements and the related deliverables and artifacts—in order to satisfy that need, or the solution.

As an agile business analyst, you no longer define your role as eliciting and analyzing requirements and producing artifacts (output). Instead, you position your team to deliver the desired outcome by keeping them focused on that outcome, building a shared understanding, and making sure decisions get made.

You no longer define the goal of your team as producing outputs; it's to reach a specific outcome. A successful team seeks to maximize outcome with minimal output. That way, you get as close to the desired change in your organization and your stakeholders' behavior as possible with the least amount of initial and ongoing work.

You are an agile business analyst when you use tried and true business analysis techniques to **build and maintain a shared understanding** of the problem your team is trying to solve. You use most, if not all, of the analysis techniques you've used before, but you use them for different reasons.

You don't use an analysis technique to produce an artifact that serves as the primary (perhaps sole) means of communication. You use analysis techniques to build and maintain shared understanding between the team and stakeholders. If you produce an artifact to remember what that shared understanding is, great.

Instead of using Visio alone at your desk, you use a whiteboard collaboratively with your team and stakeholders.

Yes, business analysts elicit and document requirements, but those activities are just means to an end. Analysis is about understanding your stakeholders and their needs, identifying the best solution for satisfying those needs in your context, and then building a shared understanding of that solution. Requirements play a part in that work, especially around describing the need, but they are certainly not the end product.

When the teams I worked with thought that the business analyst's sole responsibility was requirements, my role was diminished and I lost the ability to make sure the team delivered the right thing.

Things were different when I stepped up, sought to understand why we were working on the project in the first place, and then made sure everyone on the team had the same understanding. The project went better, I enjoyed my work a lot more, and I found I had much more influence on that project and in the organization.

You are an agile business analyst when you **make sure decisions get made**, whether you have the responsibility for deciding or not.

You are an agile business analyst when you **use short feedback cycles to learn** about your users' needs and adjust your product accordingly.

You learn at each step of the software development lifecycle. You learn about your solution when you build parts of it. You learn about your solution when you test it. You learn about your solution when customers look at it and users use it.

These are all feedback cycles, and you want them to be as short as possible so you can learn quickly and make sure you stay headed in the right direction. To make the most effective use of those feedback cycles, you don't want to get too far ahead of what's getting built next.

There's certainly value in understanding the breadth of what you're trying to deliver, but you don't want to dive deep on everything too soon. The key phrase is "a mile wide and an inch deep," followed by repeated cycles of "an inch wide and a mile deep."

Establish the general parameters of what you're going to tackle and then do deep dives on small aspects of the overall solution when you need to.

Let's take a closer look at the five things that make you an agile business analyst.

Consider context

"It depends."

The annoying, but honest, answer given to most questions about product development. If someone provides that answer and stops there, they're trying to avoid the question.

If they say that and then continue to explain what happens in various situations, they are admitting the impact of context in product development.

The impact of context prevents best practices from being a real thing. The term "best practice" frequently describes techniques or processes that were successful for one team or organization and are being copied by others.

Unfortunately, what works for one team may not work as well in your situation. Many environmental factors can play a role in the effectiveness of a practice for a given team. For this reason, I typically say "appropriate practices" or "good practices," emphasizing the fact that there really are no *best* practices across all situations.

Your team has to consider your environment, your organization, and your product when choosing which processes, practices, and techniques you'll use, so you can be sure you're doing whatever will make them successful—and skipping anything that's not necessary.

Perhaps considering context is the only real best practice.

Focus everyone on maximum outcome with minimum output

Outcomes are changes in the world that happen because of your work. With internal products, outcomes show up as changes in the organization or in your stakeholders' behavior. You deliver outputs in order to achieve some outcome. Outputs can include code, tests, requirements, and documentation.

Gojko Adzic suggests another way to describe outcomes and outputs. You can look at outputs as effort spent or invested and outcomes as what your customers get as a result of that investment.

Because outputs are typically easier to measure than outcomes, most teams and organizations measure progress and define scope by the number of outputs produced. But it's possible to produce a large number of outputs, spending a lot of money in the process, and still not reach the desired outcome.

It's better to focus on the outcome that you want, and **then as a team** determine the minimum outputs necessary to deliver that outcome. This shortens the time required to deliver the outcome, reduces the cost of producing the outcome, and decreases long-term costs, as you have fewer outputs (code, tests, documentation) to maintain.

The secret is to build a shared understanding of the problem your stakeholders are trying to solve (outcome) and then determine the most appropriate solution (output) for realizing that outcome.

Don't take all stakeholder requests verbatim; instead, dig a little deeper to understand what's behind each request. Observing people at work is a great way to dig deeper. You may not immediately know what to ask about, but you'll notice things when you watch your users.

Consider the information you get from talking with and observing your users, then decide whether the stakeholder request is relevant to your given solution. If it is relevant, determine the underlying need that the stakeholder is trying to satisfy, and tackle that need. If the request is not relevant, explain to the stakeholder why it's not appropriate to address right now.

Once you understand the outcome you're trying to deliver, as well as the assumptions underlying that outcome, use that information to guide what you do next. Select the outputs (often expressed as features) that allow you to make progress toward the targeted outcome, or that help validate assumptions. Which aspect you focus on first depends on how far along you are toward reaching the desired outcome. At first you'll spend more effort validating assumptions (you can also think of this as reducing uncertainty), then delivering features that you know provide the value you seek.

The key point here is to identify value first, then iteratively identify the features that you need to deliver that value. Don't brainstorm a big list of possible changes and then try to figure out how much "business value" each feature could contribute. Measuring value at the granularity of a user story is very difficult and wastes effort. Too often, a team spends time overanalyzing the value points associated with a story when they could easily have made a priority decision in another way. By working from outcome (value) to output (features) instead of in the other direction, you'll have fewer items to manage at any point and you'll avoid the tricky business of assigning value to any specific change.

In addition to delivering only required outputs, deliver those outputs using only necessary activities. In practice, this means that the approaches your team uses should be barely sufficient (with adjustments along the way as needed, based on experience).

Don't get too hung up on the arcane semantics of modeling techniques. You're using models to aid with communication and build a shared understanding. Imperfect is okay as long as everyone involved in the discussion understands what the model conveys. You can always chat to clear up any confusion.

Complicated processes or frameworks are rarely good ways to address complexity. The more complicated a process is, the less likely people are to follow it effectively—and, perversely, the more likely they are to hide behind the complicated process, to the detriment of the entire team. Keep your processes simple, and adjust them as you learn.

Build and maintain shared understanding

In a good collaboration, team members commit to meeting a joint goal, and they're not afraid to step outside their area of specialization to help others on the team. All team members have a specialty (such as development, testing, or analysis) on which they spend a considerable part of their time. But when the need arises, they should be able to jump in and work on something else to help the team meet its overall goals.

As a business analyst, this might involve:

- facilitating whole-team collaboration
- helping other team members improve their analysis skills
- helping other team members be more effective with discovery
- using team member and stakeholder insights to aid in analysis
- helping out with testing and documentation when other team members get stuck taking advantage of different perspectives

Don't hoard all the analysis work for yourself, or restrict your team members' contributions to it.

Make sure decisions get made

Success in many types of organizations (for-profit, not-for-profit, governmental) depends on making well-informed, timely decisions. When I've worked on successful projects in successful organizations, the one common characteristic was clear decision making. Conversely, in less successful cases, a common factor was poor (or nonexistent) decision making.

An important aspect of decision making is who makes the decisions. That person should be as informed as possible and be in a position to make the decisions stick. In many organizations, the people expected to make most decisions—senior leadership—are not the best informed; leaders may not have the in-depth knowledge required to make a good decision.

You can resolve these issues by spreading decision making throughout the organization. This helps ensure that the people with the relevant information are the ones who make certain decisions. A prime example is teams deciding the best way to approach their work, assuming they have the proper understanding of the desired outcome and understand the constraints under which they must work.

Operate in short feedback cycles to learn

Unlike operational work, internal product development rarely uses directly repeatable processes. When you're engaged in operational work, such as assembling a vehicle or processing a claim, many of the steps can be copied directly from one unit to the next. Identifying improvements becomes easier because there is very little time between cycles of a particular set of work tasks. Operational work is repetitive and fairly predictable; you can always learn how to do it better.

In contrast, no two product development efforts are alike. Even if you get the opportunity to work on multiple products, the lessons you learn from one probably aren't exactly applicable to another. You can note patterns and trends, but each experience will be a little different.

A focus on continuous learning, with iterations being a key component, reminds your team to stop every so often and figure out what they can revise. This also helps you identify meaningful milestones, with progress shown as actual working output rather than intermediate artifacts.

It's important to validate assumptions early in your project, so you can determine whether you have identified the right solution to the right problem. Asking your stakeholders for feedback is helpful but, due to the influence of cognitive biases, they could give you misleading information.

The Build-Measure-Learn loop[16] provides a way to validate assumptions in conjunction with talking to your stakeholders. It also encapsulates the overall approach to building and getting feedback, which is a key aspect of the guiding principle to reflect and adapt.

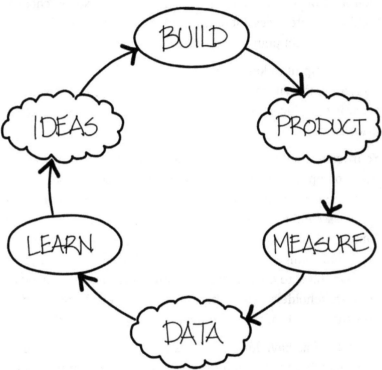

Figure 1. *The Build-Measure-Learn loop echoes Walter Shewhart's Plan-Do-Study-Act cycle but emphasizes getting through the cycle as quickly as possible so the team can validate assumptions and test hypotheses about solutions.*

---

[16] https://www.kbp.media/build-measure-learn/

Quick cycles through the Build-Measure-Learn loop can help your team reduce the uncertainty that often comes along with products. Start by tackling the biggest or riskiest assumptions. Eric Ries calls them the "leap-of-faith assumptions," but it may be easier to think of them as the assumptions that, if proven wrong, can significantly reduce the chances that you deliver the desired outcome. For example, when I was working on a recent product we identified outside as the biggest source of risk, so we chose to build those interfaces out first, even though the related data were used at different points in the overall business process.

It's also helpful to keep a mindset of identifying the right solution rather than iterating on a known solution. One way is to ask, What is our biggest unknown that would drive a change to our priority list?

Your team should continuously learn from its experiences if you want to improve your approach and your outcome. Specific projects often last longer than a couple of months. During that time, business conditions, team member understanding of the outcome, and the environment surrounding the product will all grow and change. Your team should seek to use that change to its advantage, to ensure that your outcome meets the needs of your stakeholders when the result is delivered—not just the perceived needs of the stakeholders when you started.

Project teams have long done postmortems or lessons learned sessions where team members gather at the end of the project to talk about what happened—usually the negative aspects—in hopes that they can do better next time.

If that end-of-project analysis is considered a good practice, wouldn't it make sense to do the same thing while you're working on a product, when the team still has time to make changes that affect the outcome? This is the idea behind retrospectives,[17]

---

[17] https://www.kbp.media/action-focused-retrospectives/

which provide teams with a mechanism to discuss what has transpired to date—things the team did well, along with opportunities for improvement—and decide what course corrections should be made.

A recent example

I was the product owner for the initiative to revise the Agile Alliance website, membership, and conference registration systems. When it came time to do a deep dive into the membership aspects of the system, I took it upon myself to write up all the specifics about membership— what information we wanted to track about members, what rules were relevant, and what types of memberships we had. It was a short yet comprehensive set of requirements. I was admittedly quite happy with them.

Until the delivery team started developing functionality without seeming to pay much attention to the requirements.

At first, I was perplexed. Did I not clearly tell the team where the requirements were?

Then I was irritated. Why weren't they paying any attention to my carefully crafted backlog items?

Then it occurred to me that I had focused on the requirements as an output, without considering how it contributed to our desired outcome—increased membership. I didn't talk with the delivery team to find out the best way to share information with them as they built the various aspects of the membership functionality. We didn't have conversations as we went along to point out the relevant rules and pieces of information for the specific backlog item that they were working on at the time.

So we changed how we communicated. We still used the rules and data element information, but we used them more as reference points in the frequent conversations we had. We started relying on examples as we talked through the specifics of a given backlog item. We found that it was not enough for me to simply write those examples down. In many cases, the real advantage came from talking through them as the delivery team was starting on a backlog item.

I should have known better than to start the way we did. But it's easy to forget good practices when you're in the thick of it and the pressure is on. Here are some good practices I hope you remember when you run into the same situation:

- Take time to talk with your team about how you want to work and the best way to communicate information in order to build and maintain a shared understanding. When you have those discussions, don't be afraid to suggest approaches that your team is not familiar with if they are applicable to your project.
- Document requirements collaboratively during your discussions, to build and maintain a shared understanding.
- Stop thinking of analysis in terms of gathering and capturing requirements, and instead think of it as solving problems and building a shared understanding.

One time we can talk about how

If you've been doing business analysis for any length of time, you're probably used hearing that you should focus on the what, not the how. That is true. However, when it comes to talking about being an agile business analyst, it's okay to break that rule.

We just discussed five things you need to do to be an agile business analyst. Chapters 4–11 describe in more detail how you go about doing that.

CHAPTER 4 – CONTEXT: CONSIDER YOUR ORGANIZATION'S STRATEGY

You want to understand your organization's strategy so you're clear not only about the need you're trying to satisfy but also about whether that need is worth satisfying. You can tell that by understanding how that need relates to helping your organization build and maintain a competitive strategic advantage.

Have you ever worked for an organization that has too many projects? The situation is usually characterized by endless discussions of how long this project will really take, whether the hero project manager can take on one more project, and how you could implement the newest, shiniest methodology to "leverage the synergies in your overallocated resources" (translation: burn out your employees).

I have worked at and with several organizations that face the situation described above. In most, the people at those organizations hold a specific, and entirely unstated, assumption: every project on the list Has. To. Be. Done.

You don't have to fall victim to that mindset. You can choose to be honest with yourself and your organization about how much you can get done, and productively decide which things on the list will get tackled, and which ones won't. The thing that can guide you through those difficult decisions is your organization's strategy.

Key assumptions about strategy

To show how strategy can help you, here are some observations I've made about strategy and conclusions I've formed as a result.

Observation 1: Strategy exists to guide decision making. A good strategy does not specify the exact actions that your organization is going to take (i.e., a Strategic "Plan"); rather, it provides guard rails that express the intent of your organization.

Observation 2: Effective decision making occurs when decisions are made by informed people. The most informed people tend to be the ones doing the day-to-day work because they are closest to the action, and because they aren't dealing with filtered information like those near the top of the organization chart. See Chapter 10 for more on decision making.

Observation 3: Your organization executes its strategy via projects. A well laid out strategy will have some aspects that guide decisions for day-to-day operations in your organization.

However, most strategy tends to drive change, and more often than not that change is driven through projects, even if they've adopted product based thinking.

Observation 4: If people do not understand the strategy, they will ignore it. They will also ignore the strategy if it is not actionable, or they will interpret it in a way that makes their lives easier. Strategies that are communicated by a 60-slide PowerPoint deck, that have a bunch of vague "motherhood and apple pie" statements, or that have a stunning array of goals do not aid decision making.

Conclusion: To ensure effective decision making, ensure people working on initiatives understand your organization's strategy. If you consider the observations listed above and follow where they lead, you will want to make sure that the people working on your initiatives(s) understand your organization's strategy so that they can make informed decisions consistent with your organization's intent.

Strategy needs to be simple, useful, known, and understood. Once it meets those criteria, you can use it to improve the chances of delivering the right things, assuming you are willing to have some tough conversations once in a while. Here's how.

Understand the strategy

If you don't understand the organization's strategy overall, it will be difficult to figure out how relevant your project is to that strategy. The first step here is to find out what the strategy is.

As a consultant, I'll often start by looking around the organization's intranet site to get an initial idea of the strategy. I'll follow up with a meaningful conversation with someone involved in creating the strategy (if possible), or at least someone that started the initiative I am working on.

The goal is to understand how I should use the organization's strategy to make decisions about the specific product I'm working on. If the strategy is structured properly, I'm usually able to create a decision filter[18] out of it; for example, "Will this help us do [X]?" where [X] is the intent of the organization.

If you use the decision filter approach, and if your organization's strategy can be used in that manner, you now have a good guide for making decisions about what problems you should try to solve, what features you should include or not, and how you approach designing certain features.

If it's difficult to determine a clear strategy for your organization, or if it's not stated in such a way that you can use it to easily make decisions, you may need to be a bit more intentional about how you discover your organization's strategy.

Here's an approach I've used to discover an organization's strategy, at least to the extent where I can make decisions about the

---

[18] https://www.kbp.media/decisionfilters/

projects and product I'm working on. It starts with the Purpose Based Alignment Model and supplements it with six questions to bring some clarity.

Purpose Based Alignment Model

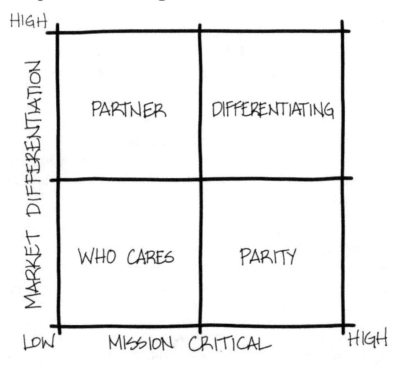

Figure 2. The Purpose Based Alignment Model provides focus by guiding decisions about which activities to concentrate on based on their value to the organization.

The Purpose Based Alignment Model,[19] created by Niel Nickolaisen, is a method for aligning business decisions and process and feature designs around purpose. The purpose of some decisions and designs is to differentiate the organization in the market; the purpose of most other decisions is to achieve and maintain parity with the market. Those activities that do not

---

[19] https://www.kbp.media/purpose-based-alignment-model/

require operational excellence either necessitate finding a partner to achieve differentiation or do not deserve much attention.

In practice, purpose alignment generates immediately usable, pragmatic decision filters that you can cascade through the organization to improve decisions and designs.

The purpose of the **differentiating** activities is to excel. Because you use these activities to gain market share and to create and maintain a sustainable competitive advantage in the marketplace, you want to perform these activities better than anyone else. For your organization, these activities are or should be its claim to fame. These activities link directly to your strategy. You should be careful to not underinvest in these activities, as that would weaken your market position. Focus your creativity on these processes.

What are the differentiating activities for your organization? It depends on the specific things you do to create sustainable competitive advantage.

The purpose of the **parity** activities is to achieve and maintain parity with the marketplace. Stated differently, your organization does not generate any competitive advantage if it performs these activities better than its competitors. However, because these activities are mission critical, you must ensure that you do not underinvest in these activities or perform them poorly. These activities are ideal candidates for simplification and streamlining, because complexity implies that you are overinvesting. While there might be value in performing the differentiating activities in a unique way, performing the parity activities in a unique way will not generate value—and could actually decrease the organization's value if your overinvestment in parity processes limits the resources you can apply to differentiating processes.

Some activities are not mission critical (for your organization) but can nevertheless differentiate the organization in the marketplace. The way to exploit these activities—and generate increased market share—is to find a **partner** for whom those activities are differentiating and combine efforts to create this differentiation.

Finally, some business activities are neither mission critical nor market differentiating. The goal for these activities is to perform them as little as possible. These are the "**who cares**" activities. Because these activities are neither market differentiating nor mission critical, you should spend as little time and attention as possible on them if you even do them at all.

Using the Purpose Based Alignment Model

When you start a new project, it's a good idea to use the Purpose Based Alignment Model to analyze the activities your product supports. If you classify those activities according to the model you can determine which ones to ignore, which ones to focus on, and how to approach those that you're doing something about.

Gather the stakeholders and key decision makers related to your product and the specific project you're working on. It's best if you can meet somewhere with a whiteboard and with plenty of stickies and markers on hand.

Draw the four quadrants on the whiteboard and explain what each quadrant means. While you're explaining the model, provide some example activities. This will prompt other ideas about activities and will allow you to provide example classifications.

If you're struggling to come up with activities, refer to the American Productivity & Quality Center (APQC) Industry Specific Process Classification frameworks.[20] The APQC also has a cross-

---

[20] https://www.apqc.org/industry-specific-process-classification-frameworks

industry version[21] that you can use if there isn't an industry specific process classification framework available. The processes listed in those frameworks are excellent examples of the type of activities you should use in your analysis. For example, some activities that would make sense to map for a health insurance provider include:

- Manage health care delivery
- Support health care management
- Adjudicate claims and process reimbursement
- Manage receipt and route of transactions
- Provide explanations of benefits (EOBs) to members

If you do choose to use the process classification frameworks as a reference, keep in mind that you don't have to use *all* the processes listed. Focus on the ones that are relevant to the product or project you're working on.

Once you've explained the model and what you mean by activities, ask the group to identify activities. If you would like to generate a lot of ideas quickly, give everyone a pile of sticky notes and ask them to individually write activities down, one activity per sticky, for a given time period (five minutes is common). Then, have each person read out the activities they came up with and put the sticky notes on a wall. This approach generates a lot of ideas, but it will also generate duplicates. Take some time to group similar ideas together and identify any that are missing.

You could also just ask the group to suggest activities while you, or a volunteer, write them on individual sticky notes. This approach may be a little quicker, but it won't generate as many activities and it could lead to less participation by the more

---

[21] https://www.apqc.org/resource-library/resource-listing/apqc-process-classification-framework-pcf-cross-industry-excel-7

reserved members of the group who may have some really good ideas.

Make sure that you end up with a collection of activities that are relevant to your product, and make sure that everyone understands what each activity means.

Once you identify the activities, you need to place them in the appropriate quadrant. A good approach to categorizing several activities quickly is a group sort technique used as part of the risk management game[22] from Ken Clyne and Steve Bockman's team estimation game.[23]

1. Gather the sticky notes together and put them in a pile.
2. Ask a volunteer to take the first sticky note off the pile and place it in the correct quadrant of the purpose based alignment model you drew on the whiteboard during your explanation.
3. Go clockwise to the next person. Give them three choices:
   - Place the next activity on the board.
   - Move an existing activity to a different category. If someone chooses this option, they should explain why they moved the activity.
   - Pass – this choice should only be used when the number of sticky notes is getting low.
4. Repeat Step 3 until all the activities have been placed on the board and everyone has passed.

Now that you have all the activities categorized, you may want to confirm the results. The primary check is whether you have identified more than three differentiating activities. Any more than that is a sign that the organization doesn't understand its competitive advantage or has no real focus.

---

[22] https://www.kbp.media/risk-management-game/
[23] http://agileworks.blogspot.com/2008/01/team-estimation-game-by-steve-bockman.html

Watch out for the tendency to equate differentiating with important. When people fall in to this trap, they will find ways of justifying whatever they are working on as differentiating. Try the billboard test: If an activity is truly differentiating, you would be willing to buy a large billboard to advertise it. If a billboard advertising the activity seems ludicrous ("buy from us because we have the most efficient time tracking"), the activity is not differentiating.

Another way to identify differentiating activities is to ask yourself six questions.[24] These six questions represent two different perspectives.

You can use the first four questions to identify differentiating activities in your organization:

1) Whom do we serve?

2) What do they want and need most?

3) What do we provide to help them?

4) What is the best way to provide this?

The final two questions prompt you to think about the implications of your differentiating activities for your organization:

5) How do we know we are succeeding?

6) How should we organize to deliver?

Once you're comfortable with how you've categorized the activities, you now have some guardrails for designing around purpose.

---

[24] https://www.kbp.media/six-questions/

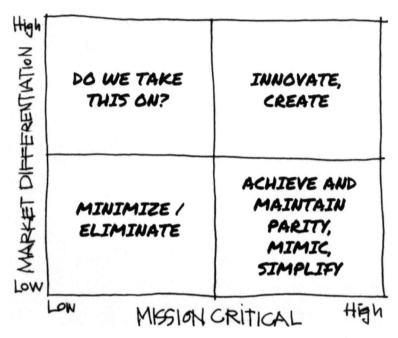

Figure 3. Knowing where an activity falls in the purpose based alignment model can help you decide how or whether to do it.

If your product supports any differentiating activities (and it may not), you should design features that support those activities with unique and creative approaches. It makes sense to be innovative in your approach to these activities.

The bulk of the activities your product supports should be parity. When you work on features that focus on these activities, design them to be good enough. Seek to simplify and streamline the processes associated with these activities. If there is an industry standard functionality (sometimes referred to as "best practice") to support the activity, it's best to use that.

Partner activities are rare, but not unheard of. If your product does support a partner activity, decide whether your organization should do the activity or work with another organization for whom that activity is differentiating.

If any activities ended up in the who cares quadrant, think long and hard about whether you should be supporting that activity at all. And if most of the activities your product supports show up in who cares, that's a sign the product may not be needed any more.

Things to remember about purpose based alignment

Parity activities are mission critical. You may associate your self-worth and value to the organization with the process and business rules you control and use. This creates a natural tendency to want your process and business rules to be "differentiating." If you don't emphasize and communicate the mission-critical nature of the parity activities, people will resist the use of the model and its associated decision filters. Alternatively, they may attempt to contort their processes so they fall into the differentiating category. This defeats the effective use of the model.

What is a differentiating activity changes over time. As soon as you introduce improvements to your differentiating activities, the market can mimic what you have done. To keep ahead of the mimics, you need a focused, working innovation process that constantly updates your roadmap with new improvements to your differentiating activities.

What is a parity activity changes over time. Best practices for your parity activities can change. As soon as a process improvement becomes the new standard, it creates a parity gap that you need to fill. Of course, to fill the gap, you can then mimic what someone else has invented. This requires an internal process to find and implement best practices.

Purpose is not priority. Purpose identifies the design goals of a process, business rule, function, or feature. It does not define the sequence in which the work on that process, rule, function, or feature must occur. That said, purpose can provide a framework for strategic and tactical planning.

Analytics can be differentiating. If you can make better decisions, particularly about your differentiating processes, you improve your ability to compete in the marketplace. Analysis that seeks to better understand your differentiating processes can also be differentiating. Not all analytics are differentiating, however. For example, a large retailer that differentiates itself through its superior supply chain management focuses its unique and differentiating analytics on the supply chain, not necessarily on sales data.

Treat exceptions like exceptions. Automating processes to handle exceptions generally adds nothing but complexity to your organization, and rarely differentiates the organization in a meaningful way. Avoid codifying exceptions as business rules.

Use strategy as a filter, not a bucket

It's always good to discuss the problem statement to reach a shared understanding about the need you are trying to satisfy with a project. The natural follow up to that discussion is to ask the hard question: Is it worth it? In other words, is that need worth satisfying at all, or is there a solution that will allow us to satisfy the need effectively?

While that seems like an easy question, it doesn't get asked as often as it should. And when it does get asked, it isn't always answered honestly. I've found a couple of approaches to ask and answer that question effectively.

Todd Little asks, "Is your strategy a filter or a bucket?"[25] Let's dive into that a little more to understand what he means.

---

[25] http://toddlittleweb.com/Strategy.html

Take a financial services organization that publishes their six "priorities" on their website:[26]

- Putting customers first
- Growing revenue
- Managing expenses
- Living our vision and values
- Connecting with communities and stakeholders
- Managing risk

If this organization treats their strategy as a *bucket*, their portfolio management approach asks someone championing a new initiative (i.e., the sponsor) to describe how that project supports one or more of those priorities in order to be considered "strategic" and improve the chances of approval. The priorities may even be listed on the initiation document template, encouraging sponsors to craft a story to force fit the initiative under one or more priorities. At this point, strategy does not aid decision making; depending on how good sponsors are at crafting stories, all initiatives could be positioned as strategic and the people responsible for making decisions about an initiative are left with no useful information.

If, however, the organization uses strategy as a *filter*, different questions are asked about a project's relation to the priorities. Instead of asking whether Project A fits into the strategy (fit the priorities), the organization asks whether Project A helps realize the priorities better than Project B or other options. The strategy is used to determine which projects are a better fit and should move forward. The other projects aren't necessarily bad ideas, they just don't help the organization achieve its targeted outcome and therefore should not be done.

I like to take things even further. If the organization reduced the number of priorities down to three or fewer, these priorities

---

[26] https://www.wellsfargo.com/about/corporate/vision-and-values/our-priorities/

could be turned into explicit decision filters expressed in the form of a question: Will this help us do X? Each project would then be assessed using those decision filters. If the sponsor can answer yes to those questions, the project continues. Projects where the sponsor can't answer yes to the decision filters are either stopped or changed so they can pass through the filter.

Using strategy as a filter aids in decision making and provides coherent focus, which is what strategy is for. You can clearly state what you will **not** do, which Michael Porter[27] called the essence of strategy.

Talking to decision makers about strategy filters

The lack of clear decisions about what not to do is the result of lack of action on behalf of decision makers in the organization. Business analysts can play a critical part in making those decisions happen. The practices suggested above are great ways to start the conversation about whether a project is worth it, both when it is launching and after it is already underway. It's important to ask probing questions, and you want to make sure that you are probing in the right places, and in the right manner.

I have found it helpful to talk to your team to understand what decision filters you should use and what objectives you should use to measure success. Then, if you realize that the project you are considering does not seem to pass those filters or to meet those objectives, have private conversations with the project sponsor about your concerns.

It's generally not a good idea to call them out in front of the whole team, especially if you want to maintain an ongoing working relationship with that sponsor. You may find you may need some help from someone who has a good relationship with the

---

[27] https://hbr.org/1996/11/what-is-strategy

sponsor, either by coaching you through the discussion ahead of time or joining the conversation. You need to ask those questions; just consider how you go about asking them.

Explore the continue/change/stop decision regularly

Ultimately, you want strategy to guide your decision to start a project, and then, on an ongoing basis, you want to use strategy to guide your decision to continue, change, or stop that project.

During retrospectives, releases, or planning discussions, reflect to make sure you are accomplishing what you should. Ask your team to consider whether the project is still heading in the right direction. Should you continue, change, or kill the project? Depending on the nature of your organization, you may need to do this anonymously. If the general direction of the team is Change, find out what changes they suggest. If the suggestion is Kill, find out why and discuss the impact.

Be prepared for the discussion with your sponsor, should the team indicate Change or Kill. The kill option will always be difficult because of the sunk cost fallacy and how it plays on people's decision making.

An example of using strategy for decisions in a not-for-profit

I used to be involved with the Greater Iowa chapter of the Juvenile Diabetes Research Foundation (JDRF). During my time on the board, I found it to be a great example of how tying initiatives to strategy can make it easier to manage those initiatives. Strategy provides a clear picture of your end goal, and guardrails that help you make day-to-day decisions on your initiatives.

JDRF has a very clear and concrete mission around which it builds its strategy—to find a cure for Type 1 diabetes and its complications through the support of research.

In our local chapter, the strategy was centered on utilizing the most effective way to raise funds for research by establishing and maintaining strong relationships with donors and volunteers. To accomplish this strategy the chapter ran three events every year: the Walk to Cure Diabetes; the Hope Gala—a black-tie dinner with silent and live auctions; and the Ride to Cure Diabetes.

Because these events were directly driven by chapter strategy, the board, staff, and volunteers understood why events happened and what the events were meant to accomplish. This was a powerful effect, because aside from a few staff members, the events were planned by teams of volunteers motivated to make the events a success to raise the most money possible to fund research to find a cure for Type 1 diabetes.

You can replicate this type of focused effort and motivation at your organization, with people paid to work on these projects, by identifying a similar tie to the organization's strategy. If you can identify what value the initiative adds to the business and communicate that clearly to the team, chances are you will have a similarly motivated team.

When considering a new initiative at JDRF, we always asked if it helped us either raise money effectively or establish and maintain relationships with our donors. It probably didn't hurt that the chapter ran with rather limited resources, and we were very selective about what new initiatives we would take on. This check back to strategy during the decision process proved very helpful, and allowed the chapter to stay focused. This is a practice that more organizations could learn from. It provides focus and prevents portfolios from exploding beyond a manageable level.

Since each event was tied back to strategy (Will this help us raise funds for research?), it was easy to quantify success. Funds raised to support research is a tangible measure of value added to the organization. Most organizations do not have such a concrete measure for every initiative, but tying those initiatives to strategy make coming up with a similarly meaningful measure that much more successful.

A powerful use of strategy for the JDRF local chapter was deciding which events *not* to do. As an example, the chapter declined an opportunity to participate in a daylong fair that focused on the treatment of diabetes. The event may have done some things to build a relationship with families impacted by diabetes, many of whom were donors, but it did not raise any funds. In fact, it required the expenditure of some funds, plus taking a great deal of staff time away from those events that did raise funds. What's more, the fair was focused on treatment, while JDRF is focused on finding a cure. Not all the volunteers who worked with the local chapter were happy with the decision, but it was the proper decision based on the chapter's strategy.

More organizations can learn from this example—sometimes you have to make tough decisions in the short term to allow your organization to stay focused in the long term.

The adage is that you have to spend money to make money, however JDRF prides itself on being one of the most efficient not-for-profits in the country. When I was involved with the chapter, roughly 85 cents of every dollar raised went straight to supporting research. This focus on efficiency, which is embedded in JDRF's strategy, influenced many of the day-to-day decisions made about the events. Here are a couple of examples.

One of the events has been held on the same weekend every year since its inception over 20 years ago. One year, the usual venue was not available because there were other events that were committing to spend more money on room rent and food costs. Even though it meant breaking with a long-held tradition, the chapter changed the date. It was more important to maintain an efficient event than to stick with the same date.

Another case involves the JDRF bike ride, where people raise money to travel to a destination and ride 100 miles in a single day. Initially, these were "destination" locations—places people like to go to for vacations. But the cost to get the riders there ate up a considerable chunk of the donations. After a couple of years, the chapter worked with other chapters and the national organization to establish a bike ride in the Midwest instead. The travel costs were lower and the amount of money raised for research increased.

The chapter also used the focus on strategy to help determine its approach to each event. The intent for the Hope Gala is to be one of the most elegant charity events in Central Iowa, but the chapter always found ways of creating that elegance in the least expensive manner possible.

Staff and volunteers expend a lot of effort getting as many services donated as possible to keep expenses low. What volunteers can't get donated they find creative ways to get discounted in exchange for positive publicity for the organizations we work with.

Most organizations aren't planning black-tie dinners and bike rides as their major initiatives but there are some parallels—primarily understanding what the project is intended to accomplish and approaching that project accordingly.

It's about honest conversations

To deliver the right thing and avoid working on the wrong things, you need a strategy that effectively guides decisions. You need to have honest conversations regarding the alignment of projects to that strategy. And you need to be willing and able to convince your sponsor that their treasured project is no longer a great idea. It may be unpleasant at first, but I think you'll find it's a much more effective approach over the long run.

Project teams should take it upon themselves when starting a project to make sure they are very clear on why the project is being done. They should be able to raise questions about whether the project is the right thing to do, or raise concerns when it seems that the project is no longer heading down the right path. These can be difficult conversations, but if they occur as soon as the team members realize something is not right, it's much easier to make the right decision to transform or kill the project. Either result is a success—much more so than burying your head in the sand and hoping no one notices that your project is building a bridge to nowhere.

Build a shared understanding of the tie to strategy with the rest of the team

Assuming you are continuing your project, you need to make sure that your team understands the strategy and the initiative's relation to it.

This is the audience participation part of the project. Your results will be better than if you merely distribute a document to the team and ask them to read it. Having people read a document is better than doing nothing, but involving them in a discussion with the sponsor is even more powerful.

A technique you may find helpful for reinforcing this tie is the problem statement. I discuss how to use the problem statement to build shared understanding of the outcome you seek in Chapter 8.

Reinforce the linkage to strategy throughout the project

As the project proceeds, your team will face decisions along the way:

- What items should we work on next?
- How should we approach this particular item?
- Should we work on more new stuff or fix the defects we run into?

When the team comes across these questions, encourage them to consider your decision filter(s) and use that to guide their decisions. See Chapter 10 for more information on decision making.

The mindset that project managers or project teams have no responsibility for making sure their projects are appropriately aligned with business objectives is unfortunately more common than I would like. I've seen several projects where many team members knew that the project was not supporting any business objectives and did not say anything or make it explicitly clear that the project faced problems. This is often a result of learned helplessness—teams convince themselves that they can't possibly have a say in deciding the importance of a project.

Chapter 5 – Context: Consider Your Organization's Structure

The structure of your organization, specifically the structure of your product teams, plays a big role in the techniques that you'll use. To fully understand how these differences influence your choice of techniques, it's helpful to look at organizational functions, how to organize product people, and how to structure product teams.

Organizational functions

You'll typically find product people in one of three functions in your organization—product management, product ownership, or business analysis. These functions have substantial overlap in their responsibilities, but each has a specific focus.

- Product management focuses on understanding an organization's customers, understanding their needs, and determining whether it's worth it for their organization to satisfy those needs. This function primarily deals with an organization's customers and users.
- Product ownership focuses on supporting the team delivering the solution and making sure that team has the information necessary to deliver the right solution effectively. This function primarily deals with the delivery team.
- Business analysis focuses on understanding the business processes and business rules necessary to satisfy your customers' needs. This function primarily deals with subject matter experts—and to some extent users.

Here's a closer look at each function and their relevance to an agile business analyst.

Product management

Melissa Perri, in her Product Institute online course,[28] describes product management as effectively solving problems for customers while achieving business goals. It's about becoming an expert in the needs of your organization's customers and identifying ways to satisfy those needs that are beneficial to your organization.

As a result, product management requires a balance between the needs of your customers and the needs of your organization.

Some product management techniques help you build and maintain a direct, meaningful connection with your organization's customers. Other product management techniques help you to assess those needs against your organization's strategy and business plan. Still other techniques help you make decisions about what problems to solve and what products to build and update.

Product management also deals with the business aspects of selling the product and making it available to your organization's customers.

In an external product context, product management is often the function that incorporates everything product people do. Product ownership, then, is a subset of product management and business analysis doesn't necessarily exist as a separate function.

In an internal product context, there may not be an explicit product management function. The connection with customers and decision-making activities usually occur in various business units (or, in more cases than I care to admit, decision-making responsibility does not seem to rest anywhere).

---

[28] https://productinstitute.com/

If you are an agile business analyst in an organization with an explicit product management function, you'll want to get clear on your relationship with it (if you're not explicitly part of it). If your organization does not have a definitive product management function, you'll want to gain clarity and build shared understanding around where the key product management activities take place. You may also need to be prepared to fill the gaps if you identify some.

In addition, a key part of being an agile business analyst is behaving as if you are in a product management function. This is especially the case when it comes to decision making and working on the right things. If you can, keep a constant focus on working on the right problems and not working on everything else. Make the decisions every day that allow you and your team to focus on the things that should be done to solve problems for your customers and achieve business goals.

If you do not have that decision-making authority, make sure that you can influence the people that do to focus on solving the right problems. This could be different behavior than you're used to, but it's essential to adding value to your organization.

And if you find you don't have that type of influence because of the characteristics of your organization, that may be a sign it's time for a change.

Product ownership

The product ownership function was originally created to describe the activities that the product owner role does in the Scrum framework. Because Scrum was created to guide the work of a software development team, the product ownership function tends to focus on what a software development team expects their product person to do. You can see this focus in the definition of product owner in the Scrum Guide.[29]

---

[29] https://www.scrumguides.org/scrum-guide.html

As a result, product ownership focuses almost entirely on the relationship with the team developing a solution. The related techniques provide clear direction regarding the right things to build and include things such as creating backlog items, refining the backlog, and providing information about backlog items. What often gets left unsaid is how product owners go about making those decisions, or how much they should look externally to understand the market.

The creation of the product owner role has caused some angst and confusion in product circles. Should there be a product manager and product owner? Should there be only one? If both, who leads whom?

Your answer to those questions will vary based on the size of your organization and whether you associate more with the product management community (product ownership is one of the many things that product managers do) or the Scrum community (sure, product owners do product management stuff too, but what really matters is that every team has a product owner). Those different answers are encapsulated in the models I describe below.

In external product contexts, you'll often see product management absorb product ownership responsibilities or split responsibilities where product ownership still reports in through the product management function.

In internal product contexts, especially those without a distinct product management function you'll often see people filling a product owner role, but not always doing it very effectively. You'll frequently find someone from the business unit that "owns" the internal product asked (or voluntold) to be product owner.

These people rarely have proper background to be effective at product ownership, except for subject matter knowledge and decision-making responsibility. They also usually keep their other responsibilities, which means that they are not available to nearly the extent that the development team desires.

As an agile business analyst, you'll want to understand how your organization approaches product ownership and you'll need to be prepared to fill gaps. Depending on the availability of your product owner, you may find yourself fleshing out backlog items, you may find yourself filling most product owner responsibilities, or you may be asked to be the product owner.

In a project I worked on recently I acted as product owner in all ways but title, key decisions, and some approval activities, because the person who had been asked to be a product owner had an entire other full-time job. The situation worked for us because we had a good working relationship and a large amount of trust. I also made it a point to keep the product owner informed continuously about what the team was doing and checked in with them on all key decisions.

Business analysis

The International Institute of Business Analysis (IIBA) describes business analysis[30] as "the practice of enabling change in the context of an enterprise by defining needs and recommending solutions that deliver value to stakeholders." In some respects, you could interpret that as product management applied to internal products.

In practice, however, there are some key differences. Most business analysis functions are in a position to support decision making but not necessarily make the decisions. One advantage of moving to a product perspective is changing this such that business analysis functions are better positioned to influence and even make key decisions.

---

[30] https://www.iiba.org/standards-and-resources/glossary/

The main activity that differentiates business analysis from product management and product ownership is the focus on understanding business processes, data, and business rules.

As an agile business analyst, you more than likely are a member of your organization's business analysis function. You need to build on your ability to understand business processes, data, and business rules. You need to make key decisions about what needs to satisfy and how to satisfy them.

How to organize product people

There are a variety of ways that organizations can structure their product people. I've found that there are four models that describe how product people are organized. The differences between the models come down to determining who interacts with customers, users, and the delivery team.

I use a sibling analogy to describe the four models. This analogy provides convenient names to reference each model and reflects the peer relationship that the people in these models usually exhibit.

- Only Child (a single product person)
- Identical Twins (product manager and product owner)
- Fraternal Twins (product manager and business analyst)
- Triplets (product manager, product owner, and business analyst)

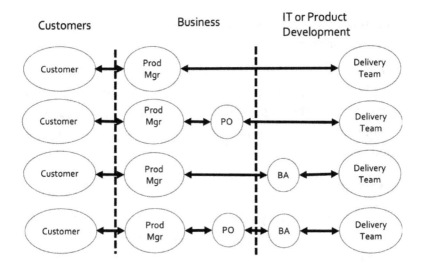

Source: Todd Little

Figure 4. *Product people organize in four different ways, depending on who interacts with customers, users, and the delivery team.*

Only Child: Single product person

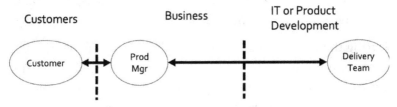

Figure 5. *In the Only Child model, a single product person interacts with both customers and the delivery team.*

Description

In this model, there is a single product person, I'll use the role product manager, that interacts both with customers and the delivery team. When you combine these roles, they identify the need; establish and maintain a roadmap; establish global and local priorities; clarify the need; describe and clarify the solution;

and communicate across a wider audience, including customer service, marketing, etc.

The product manager identifies the desired outcome, establishes the relevant metric(s), and keeps everyone focused on that outcome. They also need to build a shared understanding around that outcome, and make all the pertinent product-related decisions.

An example

This model explains my work as product owner for the Agile Alliance Submission System and website, as well as all the work I do on my KBP.media site.

At Agile Alliance, while there are stakeholders (Agile Alliance staff, the program teams working on the conferences) and users (subscribers, members, and visitors to the website and users of the submission system), at the end of the day I decide what gets done or not within the identified constraints (primarily budget, but also timeframes). I should note that I don't decide what the constraints are; those decisions are made by the Agile Alliance executive director and the board.

During the initial website construction, I didn't spend as much time with the team developing the site as I should have. This wasn't because I was spending too much time talking to customers; it was because I was doing other work. (Product ownership for Agile Alliance was not my full-time job at that moment.)

That situation is analogous to when someone from a business unit is expected to do product ownership for an internal product but is not relieved from their "day job" responsibilities. You may be able to get away with that if the team has a great deal of domain knowledge. But as I found out, if you work with a team that is outside the organization or new to that domain, you really do need a constant product ownership presence.

What this means for agile business analysts

If you find yourself in this situation (the only product person working on an internal product) you are likely doing something which is more properly described as product management than business analysis.

That might look like this list of activities described in "So you want to be a product manager? This is how I got started":[31]

- Collecting feedback from users, prioritizing it based on business impact and consumer impact, and sharing the information with relevant decision makers who can make changes happen.
- Coming up with a new idea for a feature and detailing out all the things it would do, then figuring out whether it can be built.
- Analyzing data from your website / app to determine common user paths or whether certain business events had a major impact.
- Managing revenue or profit and loss lines for a specific product or service and making changes that increase that revenue (or at least determining the impact of your internal product on revenue and profit or loss).
- Leading a project from start to finish that involves people from different teams coming together to build something.

This is a great position to be in if you want to get a good understanding of what it really means to work in product and you want to maximize influence in your organization.

---

[31] https://www.freecodecamp.org/news/how-to-break-into-product-management-d354944308c0/

Identical Twins: Product manager and product owner

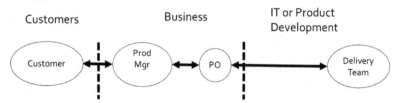

Figure 6. In the Identical Twins model, two people split the product responsibilities, one handling customer issues and the other interacting with the development team.

Description

In this model, product responsibilities are split between two people, both from the business area. One person is the product manager and focuses on market/customer concerns (more strategic, more external) and another person spends the majority of their time with the team, so they are more product and development focused (more tactical, more internal).

A key difference between this model and the Fraternal Twins model is that the product manager and product owner both "sit" in the business unit—whether that's a product management organization or a business unit that owns the process an internal product supports.

The key to making this model work is ensuring the product manager and product owner are closely aligned on the work that is supposed to happen and the aim of the product. It also requires a clear understanding about who can make different types of decisions, and trust that the product owner will accurately represent the product manager's viewpoint and plans for the product during interactions with the team.

The product manager owns establishing a roadmap and generally talks about features and benefits, while the product owner is responsible for implementing items on the backlog and talks a little about features but generally deals with user stories.

Product manager responsibilities:

- Identify the need
- Define success
- Establish and maintain roadmap
- Prioritize globally
- Confirm progress toward outcome
- Product owner responsibilities:
- Prioritize locally
- Clarify need
- Describe and clarify solution

An example

In a product company I worked with, there is a product management organization with both product managers and product owners separate from engineering. The product managers focused on the market, interacting with customers, and prioritizing features. The product owners spent most of their time interacting with the teams. There is an implied career progression from product owner to product manager.

When the organization switched to agile, they were short on product owners, so this gap was filled by either bringing product owners in from engineering or hiring them from the outside. The ones hired from the outside were familiar with agile approaches but not so much the product, which caused some issues.

In an internal product situation, the person sitting in the role resembling a product manager (probably better labeled the business leader) was the manager of the area where work was being done. Then, depending on the focus of a certain part of the project, a product owner was pulled from that business leader's staff as the product owner. They were able to make a few decisions, but were there mostly for detailed information and to answer questions.

Basically, the business leader didn't have the time to spend with the team, so she delegated that responsibility to someone who could.

What this means for agile business analysts

If you find yourself in this model you are more than likely filling the product owner role, meaning you're the main conduit between the team and other internal stakeholders needed to deliver an effective solution.

To be effective in this model, establish a good relationship with the person filling the product management role and, as much as possible, establish a good relationship between the product manager and the team. Just because you're there to be the main conduit to the team does not mean that you should shut the product manager off from all access.

You have an advantage when it comes to establishing a strong relationship with the product manager because you both report up through the same organization. That also means that you may run into a little more difficulty establishing a relationship with the team depending on how the two organizations historically collaborated.

When you find that you're in this model, have explicit discussions with the product manager to agree on who is doing what. You can use the responsibilities laid out above as a starting point, but you need to make sure you arrive at an arrangement that is the best fit for your particular context.

Fraternal Twins: Product manager and business analyst

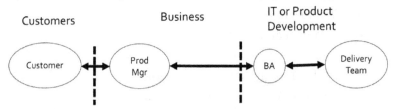

Figure 7. *The Fraternal Twins model uses an IT business analyst to interface with the delivery team instead of a business product owner, while the product manager owns customer interactions.*

Description

This model is very similar to the Identical Twins model, except that the person filling the product owner role is a business analyst in the IT organization. In this model, the product responsibilities are split between the product manager and business analyst.

This model often occurs in internal product situations where IT is working on a specific product for one or more business units but the business unit does not have, or does not value having, someone on their staff involved on a day-to-day basis with the delivery team.

This model also tends to appear when there are multiple business units impacted by work on a product and multiple "product managers"—who in this case are better described as business leaders or stakeholders. The person filling this product owner role has a very difficult job because they have to make sure that decisions happen, which often means trying to get a group of people with potentially competing needs and interests to agree—or at least agree not to disagree too much.

I have not seen this model show up in product organizations, but am curious to hear if any cases exist out there.

Product manager responsibilities:

- Identify the need
- Define success
- Establish and maintain roadmap
- Prioritize globally
- Confirm progress toward outcome
- Business analyst responsibilities:
- Prioritize locally
- Clarify need
- Describe and clarify solution

An example

Most of the projects I worked on in financial services and insurance fit this model. IT (or a separate project management office or portfolio management office) owned responsibility for launching a project and coordinating its activities. Usually, a business unit had requested the project initially and a manager or director from that business unit filled the role of business leader (the internal product version of a product manager), but they did not have time in their schedule to be with the delivery team on a regular basis. The business unit may offer up subject matter experts in some situations, but those experts are not in a position to make decisions, nor are they freed up enough to spend all of their time with the team.

Another common occurrence is a project that impacts several business units, but none of the business units want to own the product. A project to add a specific service to a data warehouse is a prime example. Several business units gain benefit from the product, but no one wants to own it. In that case, product ownership responsibilities fall to the business analyst in IT, and they often get very close to owning the business leader responsibilities as well—except they don't. The biggest risk with this type of project is that it can be extremely difficult to get decisions made because everyone approaches the project with their own interests. This type of project is also likely to experience a scope explosion.

What this means for agile business analysts

Most of the advice given for the identical twins model applies here, with the caveat that you and the product manager(s) work in different organizations so there may be some politics to work through when you establish that relationship.

The good news is that it might be easier to build a relationship with the teams since you work in the same part of the organization.

Triplets: Product manager, product owner, and business analyst

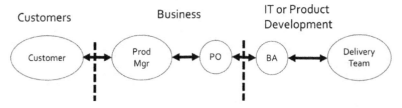

Figure 8. The inefficient but common Triplets model splits product responsibilities between three (or more) people or roles.

Description

In this model, product responsibilities are split between three or more roles: a product manager and a product owner in the business, and one or more business analysts who report up through IT or product development. This model has some inefficiencies but it is quite common, especially in internal product settings.

Typically, the product manager is a business leader in the area that the product supports. The product owner is a staff member in that same organization and usually provides subject matter expertise and connection to other staff. The day-to-day work of backlog maintenance (identifying stories and clarifying stories) falls to the business analysts.

Product manager responsibilities:

- Identify the need
- Define success
- Establish and maintain roadmap
- Prioritize globally
- Confirm progress toward outcome
- Product owner responsibilities:
- Prioritize locally
- Provide subject matter expertise
- Clarify need
- Business analyst responsibilities:
- Create and describe stories
- Describe and clarify solution

Examples

Centralized IT teams as service providers

A financial services company I worked with had a central IT organization as well as an IT function in each of the business units. The centralized IT organization adopted agile and was positioned as an option for the business units, who could either have IT work done within their own units or "hire" a team from the centralized IT area to do their work.

If a business unit engaged a team from the centralized IT unit, a member of the business unit would collocate with the team to take on product owner responsibilities. This product owner prioritized the backlog and provided subject matter expertise. While these product owners sat with the centralized team and were available to answer questions, they also maintained aspects of their day job.

Each team also had one or more business analysts who created and fleshed out backlog items. There were a couple reasons for this setup. First, the product owner may not have had much background in working with requirements and they may not have had time to fully flesh out backlog items for the team. Second, most business units produced sizable requirements documents before sourcing the work. The business analysts on the teams converted those specifications into product backlog items.

This is a classic example of what many people call Water Scrum Fall—detailed, in-depth analysis is done up front, development and testing are done iteratively, and the product may be released all at once. In most projects I saw at this organization, the product owner who sat with the team was responsible for low-level prioritization, but there was still a business leader in the business who made the broader prioritization decisions. Each engagement didn't necessarily have its own roadmap; rather, each project was launched as a roadmap item.

IT project team

Another financial services organization I worked with applied this model in a slightly different manner. The project was one of the organization's first attempts to apply agile. The people who worked in IT were organized into skill-based silos—developers separate from testers separate from analysts, etc. For this project, people were pulled from the different silos and combined into a team. But in a departure from other projects this organization had run, the team members were generally focused entirely on this project.

The leader of the business unit the project supported filled the product management role, making global prioritization decisions. She also identified a member of her staff to play the product owner role and provide more day-to-day subject matter expertise and occasional local decisions. The person filling the product owner role changed from time to time, depending on which part of the process the team was working on. The product owner generally did not collocate with the team and maintained their normal responsibilities.

One interesting twist with this team was that these product owners eventually ended up running the demos. This was done in part to make sure the product owners were familiar with the changes being made, and because the demos were used to get the rest of the staff familiar with the impending changes. The thought was that if the product owner did the demo, rather than a developer, the rest of the staff would react more positively to the change.

The team also included business analysts who were responsible for maintaining the backlog— both creating and further clarifying backlog items. They were on the team because the product owner did not have the time to perform these activities and because they did not have a wealth of analysis skills that they could call on to effectively flesh out the backlog.

What this means for agile business analysts

If you find yourself in this structure and are playing the business analyst role, you will most likely be expected to focus on the details of specific backlog items. You will spend most of your time determining how the solution will work within existing business processes, rules, and data. If the business processes, rules, or data are particularly complex this probably makes a great deal of sense.

If on the other hand, the processes, rules, and data are all fairly straightforward you may want to suggest changing to another model. There's no need for three product people for a given team if the domain is clear-cut.

It could be that the person designated as a product owner is really a subject matter expert and you can take on some of the prioritization activities that the product owner would do, or that there is another effort that is in more need of your particular set of skills.

Many in the product management space don't think you should split up the connections between customers and the team by two people, let alone three, so this model is probably one that should be used rarely. As strange as it sounds, you will prove your value to the organization by pointing out an ineffective structure and suggesting productive ways of changing that structure.

If you find the model makes sense for your context, it's essential that you build the strongest relationship possible between the three product people and have clarity around who will make what decisions.

How to structure product teams

The above discussion covers how product people are organized. Let's take a look now at how the teams they work with are structured. As you would expect, these topics intersect, which adds an entirely new level of complexity.

There is no one right way to organize the people who are doing product development, but it doesn't stop teams from looking for that silver bullet product team structure.

Marty Cagan described the three kinds of teams[32] and which kind of team is truly empowered:

- Delivery teams (aka "Scrum teams"): These teams are usually a group of developers working with a product owner (or business analyst) who works primarily as a

---

[32] https://svpg.com/product-vs-feature-teams/

backlog administrator. The team is focused almost exclusively on producing output and has little to no say or insight into what outcomes they are trying to deliver. This is, unfortunately, the most common type of team.

- Feature teams: These teams include product, design, and engineering. The team may be focused on outcomes, but they are told the best way to reach those outcomes via a prioritized list of features or projects known as the roadmap.
- Product teams: These teams include product, design, and engineering and are focused on and measured by outcomes. They are also empowered to figure out the best way to solve problems. This is what all teams should strive to be when they grow up.

Delivery teams are what you see in feature factories—feature teams are handed solutions to develop (and told why), product teams are asked to solve problems.

It occurred to me while reading Marty's post that the vast majority of internal product teams fall into the delivery team model. Part of the reason could be that most of those organizations aren't "true tech-product companies." Part of the reason could be that the result of these teams' work is not directly sold to their organization's customers.

Does that mean that teams working in this context can't be empowered? I'm not convinced.

If your team works in an internal product situation it can still be empowered if you (in Marty's words) "solve problems in ways our customers love, yet work for our business."

This may mean that you enable processes that do this. It may mean that you build the website or apps that help your organization solve problems. It may mean that you build products that provide the right environment for others in your organization to be able to focus on solving your customers' problems.

Of course, it's not just up to the teams. Your organization needs to change to provide your team more control over what you work on and how you approach that work. Is that change easy? No.

Are there many organizations making the necessary changes? No, not yet. But I'm not convinced it's impossible.

To help you start thinking about how you can get to empowered product teams inside your organization, let's look at three possible product team structures as described by Rich Mironov.

One of the key responsibilities of product leaders is to design, build, and nurture product teams. Here is what Rich calls a good product team structure, a not so good product team structure, and a really bad product team structure.

A good product team structure

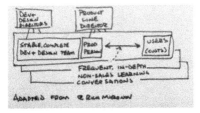

Figure 9. A good product team structure allows one product person to balance interactions with the users and the development team. Drawing adapted from work by Rich Mironov.

A product team structure that Rich likes is one in which a product person (a product manager, product owner, or business analyst—title isn't important) has about the same amount of interaction with users/customers and a team. "Team" in this case means a stable, focused cross-functional team that has all the skills needed to create the product (or part of the product) that the team is charged with delivering.

The interaction the product person has with customers and users is for the purpose of learning about their problems and any constraints around the solution. In an internal product situation, those interactions are not about users and stakeholders telling the product person what solution to build. In an external facing situation, those interactions are not sales calls.

When your product gets too big for one product person to handle the entire product with one team, you create valuable slices of the product. Each slice has its own team and a product person who can spend an equal amount of time with the team and talking to customers.

This embodies the "only child" model described above.

A not so good product structure

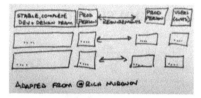

Figure 10. *In this less optimized structure, the product people speaking to customers are isolated from those working with teams, risking inefficiencies and miscommunication. Drawing adapted from Rich Mironov.*

The good thing about this product structure is that you still have stable, focused cross- functional teams with all the skills that you need to deliver your product.

The not so good part is that the product people talking to users or customers are separated from the product people working with the team.

In this model, you run the risk of a disconnect between user problems and the solution that your team puts together. You also lose much-needed context when trying to understand why your users face the problems they do and why it's valuable to solve them.

You may be able to overcome the game of telephone your product people are forced to play in this situation, but only if your product people can work very well together. If you have a choice, it's probably better to go with the structure suggested above.

I've seen (and been a part of) many teams structured in this fashion. This is the identical twin or fraternal twin model I described above.

A particularly dysfunctional application of this structure is often employed for internal products, when an organization pulls a subject matter expert from the business unit to be the product owner, but doesn't allow that person to focus on *being* a product owner. Because this product owner has to fulfill their regular duties, they spend limited time with the team, often barely talk to users or customers, and generally don't have a lot of general product management knowledge. The result? Often, someone who does have experience as a product person works closely with the team, but is unable to have meaningful conversations with users and customers.

A bad product structure

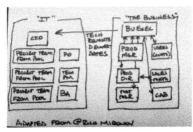

Figure 11. *This dysfunctional product team structure prevents the product person from having any direct contact with either the users or the team, which in turn prevents the team from having any real understanding of the problem they're solving or the best possible solutions. Drawing adapted from Rich Mironov.*

Unfortunately, this model probably looks painfully familiar.

Gone is the stable, focused cross-functional team with all the necessary skills. In its place is a group of people who happen to be working on the same project, some of the time. Chances are, they work on three or four others as well.

Gone is any direct relationship between the team and its users/customers.

Gone is any idea of solving a problem or of the team having the flexibility to identify potential solutions.

This structure reinforces the pattern of product people and teams as short-order cooks asking "What do you want?" and delivering exactly what the business unit executive tells them.

When the team involved is pulled from "resource pools" instead of being truly cross-functional, the model where the head of a business unit gets named as product owner becomes this model.

This structure is so undesirable that I didn't even include it in one of the models I explored for product ownership. If you find yourself in an organization that still operates in this fashion, your best bet may be to polish up your resume.

CHAPTER 6 – CONTEXT: CONSIDER YOUR PRODUCT

Say you're working on a product that you're going to sell. Do you know what problem you're solving and for whom you're solving it? Are you selling to individual consumers or to a few large organizations? Are you familiar with these buyers? Depending on the answers to these questions, you may face quite a bit of uncertainty. You'd be well served to use the product management techniques necessary to understand your customers and their needs.

Say you're working on an internal product—something you won't sell that will be used inside your organization. You need a general understanding of how this product will help your organization serve its customers, but you also need to understand your organization's processes, rules, and data. Business analysis techniques are helpful here.

You may find yourself working on your organization's website or mobile app (also internal products as I use that term). It's something your customers are going to use to buy your product and it's also something that helps people inside your organization with their activities. You'll need to understand your customers and your organization's processes in this case. You'll want to use the kind of techniques that product managers use.

Defining internal products

An internal product is software that your organization does not offer for sale to others, but instead uses to support its various business activities. Internal products can be things your organization built in-house or purchased to configure and customize (although hopefully not too much).

Internal products generally satisfy the needs of users inside your organization or enable your organization to satisfy the needs of its customers.

You can group internal products into the following general categories:

- Digital transformation (websites and apps that expose business processes to customers)
- Back office (internally developed applications that support a business process in a unique way)
- Commercial off-the-shelf (COTS) systems (CRM, ERP, HRIS)
- Business intelligence
- Maintenance and support

The specific internal products your organization has depend on the nature of your organization.

Why distinguish internal products?

I've adopted the term "internal product" to emphasize the switch to a product approach for maintaining an organization's IT assets like those listed above.

I've also adopted the term to encourage people working on those assets to apply the more intense customer focus that is more prevalent in product management circles than in many IT organizations.

Even though it seems at first glance that people inside organizations do not have a choice as to what systems they use, that isn't always the case. Business units can, and do, choose to go outside for their software tools.

Where an IT organization has successfully locked the rest of the organization into specific tools, those users may use those tools ineffectively or create inefficient work-arounds to a poorly conceived system.

Internal product management is a subset of product management with a more focused outcome and output. The outcome of internal product management is solving problems of organizational users or enabling your organization to satisfy customer needs. The output of internal product management is products that your organization does not offer for sale to others, but rather uses to support its various business activities.

Some different contexts

To see how the nature of your internal product impacts your approach, here's a look at five different contexts and how you may want to vary your approach.

Digital transformation

There are a lot of different perspectives on what digital transformation is. I describe it as applying technology to allow your customers to engage directly with your business processes in order to improve their experience. In other words, using your website and mobile apps to let your customers interact directly with your organization in ways they haven't been able to before.

What does that mean for product people in general and business analysts in particular? Product people play a significant role in digital transformations because successful digital efforts require an understanding of the customers and their needs. This **is** product management.

Activities done under the guise of digital transformation meld the customer-facing aspect of Business to Consumer (B2C) products with the need to understand your business process that is common to most IT work.

Your customers don't have to use the products you put together as part of a digital transformation, so you need to understand their needs and design a solution that they will want to use. This is where some of the most common product management and user experience practices come into play. You need to understand the customer journey. You need to know the characteristics of your customers so you know when they are most likely to use your product.

At the same time, you need to have a solid understanding of your organization's business processes, rules, and data to know how to incorporate a customer-facing interface. You need to be able to harness those business analysis skills to understand how everything fits together. You'll also find opportunities to improve the business process you're working on.

Improving a business process as part of a digital transformation

When you work in an internal product setting, you'll often get the opportunity to revisit existing business processes and look for ways to make them more effective. This usually involves finding ways to improve the interactions your customers have with those processes and automating some or all of the process.

Sometimes that work is considered part of a digital transformation.

What you call it is not necessarily important. The key is to approach the work in a way that allows you to improve the business process in a way that allows you to deliver more value to your customers.

Here's how you can use some techniques described previously on KBP.media[33] to improve business processes in a way that

---

[33] https://www.kbp.media/technique-briefs/

adds value to your customers and streamlines the business process for your organization.

These techniques help you build a shared understanding about what you're trying to accomplish and about the business process itself. Once you understand that, you can collaborate to identify areas for improvement in the business process.

Identify a metric to determine impact

When you want to improve a business process, you should start with defining what "improve" means.

How will you know that the business process is better? You could view improving a business process to mean that the process is more efficient or less expensive, but that is short-sighted. You don't want to make your business process so efficient and inexpensive that you place the entire burden of activity on your customer. If you've ever fallen into an endless phone tree loop or been lost in a poorly designed online request form, you know what I mean.

An improved business process is one that provides more value to your customers. To know that you're doing that, it can help to have some way to measure success.

You need an outcome based metric.[34] Ideally that metric represents a meaningful impact for your customers that aligns with how your organization wants to operate.

Some situations lend themselves to outcome based metrics more than others, but it's always worth trying to identify one. When you have a metric you can measure frequently, you can see whether the changes you're making are having the intended impact.

At the Agile Alliance, one example of an outcome based metric may be the amount of time it takes for someone who submits a conference session proposal to get helpful feedback. A unique aspect of the submission process for Agile Alliance conferences

---

[34] https://www.kbp.media/outcome-based-metrics/

is that the team selecting the sessions for a conference provides feedback to submitters and an opportunity to revise their session proposal. This feedback process is only valuable for the submitter if they get timely, helpful feedback.

So if the program team wanted to improve the feedback process and determines that timely feedback is an indication of a good process, they could establish the following outcome based metric:

Table 1. Example of an outcome based metric.

Name	Session Feedback Percentage
Units	The percentage of sessions submitted that receive feedback within 48 hours of requesting feedback
Method	(Count of sessions where feedback was posted within 48 hours of submitter requesting feedback/total count of sessions)
Target	90%
Constraint	65%
Baseline	65%

If the program team decides that actionable feedback is another important aspect of a good business process, they may also decide to track the percentage of feedback that the submitter marks as helpful.

Map the business process as it currently exists

Once you have a shared understanding about what it means to improve the business process and have a way to know if your actions are improving it, you can make sure everyone agrees what the process looks like currently.

You want to collaboratively create a process model[35] with the right group of people. In the case of the feedback process, that group might include a few members of the program team that play different roles (program chair, track chair, reviewer, and submitter) as well as the product team.

In an ideal world, you're able to have this discussion at a whiteboard so you can use sticky notes and markers to model the process. If you have to do it remotely, it's helpful to find a modeling tool such as Lucidchart or Visio.

Be explicit about the process you're trying to improve and where it begins and ends. In the case of the feedback process, the program team may say the process starts when someone asks for feedback on a session proposal, and ends when someone on the program team provides feedback in the submission system.

Choose the most common path through the process and identify the actions and decisions that occur. Use sticky notes to represent the actions and decisions and connect those sticky notes by drawing arrows. The feedback process is straightforward in terms of specific actions. A submitter asks for feedback, appropriate members of the program team get notified, and then one or more program team members go to the session proposal and provide feedback. This simple flow provides a good basis to have discussions about variations that might happen.

Once you've walked through the most common scenario, identify others and adjust the process model as you walk through

---

35 https://www.kbp.media/process-model/

those new scenarios. Usually, different scenarios drive new decision points or additional paths off existing decisions. In the case of the feedback process, the program team may discuss different ways that program team determines who provides feedback. For example, should only one person provide feedback initially, or can multiple people jump in?

Select a couple of examples to walk through the process. These examples may represent one of the scenarios you had already identified, or they may represent slight variations. With the feedback process, you may walk an actual example where only one person provides feedback and one when multiple people provide feedback.

When you feel like you've captured the current state take a picture of the process model, but wherever possible try to keep the original. It will be useful when you start to identify improvements.

Identify opportunities for improvement

Once you've identified the current state, you're ready to identify opportunities for improvement. Give the people involved with your discussion different colored sticky notes than the ones used to map the process. Ask them to identify all the opportunities for improvement on the business process, write those ideas on the sticky notes, and place them at the appropriate place on the process model. These sticky notes represent potential product backlog items.

In the case of the feedback process, the program team may identify different ways to notify program team members, or they may identify changes in how they use the submission system that do not require any software changes, such as a commitment to check the submission system once a day.

Once your team has identified potential backlog items, ask them to walk the model and see if there's anything missing, if they see any duplicates, or if they have questions on anything. Have the appropriate discussions and add or consolidate backlog items as needed.

When you feel you've identified the relevant product backlog items, guide a conversation to prioritize the product backlog items. You may choose to do this via dot voting or by discussing the potential items in comparison to each other. This step allows you to focus on only the backlog items that are essential to accomplishing your desired outcome.

Implement and measure

Select a product backlog item, deliver that item, give it enough time to have some effect, and then compare the current value of your chosen metric with your target and constraint. Did you reach your target? Then you can stop working on that business process and move to something else.

Did you make progress toward the target, but didn't reach it? Identify the next possible solution you could try in addition to the one you just delivered.

Did you hit the constraint level? Back out the solution you just tried and try something else, or stop work on the effort.

In the feedback process example, the team may determine that the notification emails get lost in their email boxes so they want notifications to go to the team Slack workspace. The product team makes the appropriate changes, and then the program team tries it out for a week, noting the Session Feedback Percentage right before the change was deployed and a week later. They find that the Session Feedback Percentage went from 65% to 70%. The program team could conclude that the changed helped, but other changes are needed. Those changes could be further code changes, or the team could look for changes in their work practices.

Back office

Back office work is the term I use for any internal product that an organization develops for use by internal staff to support a business process. Examples include home-grown claims administration software for an insurance company, applications used to generate pricing, and even the Agile Alliance Conference Submission System.

These products are quite common in IT organizations. They may also be the most unnecessary. When you develop a one-off product to support some business process, you inherently make the assumption that the business process is unique enough that you can't use an existing solution.

Remember the product based alignment model discussed earlier in this chapter? One key observation of that model is that the vast majority of things an organization does are parity activities. The best way to address parity activities is to mimic others or simplify them. In today's world, that can often be done by using an existing product, usually delivered by Software as a Service (SaaS) which I discuss in the next section.

Building a custom internal product for a parity activity is treating that activity as if it were differentiating, and is a waste of time and money.

That's not to say that you shouldn't do any custom development. You should focus those efforts on differentiating activities. If you can cut down on the amount of custom development you do, you'll be able to spend more effort on digital transformation efforts, or you can spend more time tying your outside services together in order to provide your staff more information.

To be fair, a lot of custom application work occurred when there weren't as many viable alternatives out in the market. It's understandable that organizations had to build their own applications; they didn't have a choice.

Now that there are a wide range of products supporting just about every common business process, it's worth considering whether you should continue to spend time maintaining those existing systems or move to a more widely available solution.

You may have to revise your business process, but chances are, that act will allow you to incorporate some industry-proven improvements.

There will still be some cases where you will want to do custom development, whether it's to create a new internal product or replace an existing system. Chapter 12 discusses the approach for building a new internal product in detail. But rebuilding an existing product does have some interesting aspects that warrant a closer look here.

How to start rebuilding an existing product

If you spend any significant time working on internal products, you're eventually going to get the opportunity to rebuild an existing product.

These types of projects have the advantage of a great deal of information about the problem you're trying to solve and a possible solution.

Sometimes you need to dig for that knowledge and be able to separate what people think the current product does and why from what the product actually does.

You also need to resist the urge to just rebuild exactly what you already have while incorporating the odd user wish list item here and there.

You want to think about how you would go about solving the problem you identify with the benefit of all you know about the problem from the years of using the existing system.

Here are the techniques I use when starting an effort to replace an existing system. They help you walk the delicate balance between understanding the current state and staying focused on solving a problem, not just recreating the same old system.

Use the problem statement to identify your desired outcome

Let me clarify something right off the bat. You are trying to solve one or more problems with the current situation. It could be that the current system is no longer supportable. It could be that the business process has changed so much that the existing product no longer supports it. It could be both those things and more.

In order to find out the real reason you're rebuilding an internal product, do the problem statement exercise[36] with your team. It will ensure you have clarity on your desired outcomes, and it will help your team get a shared understanding of those desired outcomes.

Establish criteria to help you make decisions

As part of your discussion about outcomes, use the result of the problem statement exercise to determine 1–3 decision filters.[37]

Explore the interfaces you currently have and would like to have

Any product that's worth rebuilding most likely interfaces with at least a few other products, and at the very least is used by multiple people or departments in your organization. Use a context diagram[38] to understand those current interactions and identify potential future interactions. You can also use the context diagrams to identify interfaces that are manual today that you may want to automate in the future.

---

[36] https://www.kbp.media/problem-statement/
[37] https://www.kbp.media/decisionfilters/
[38] https://www.kbp.media/context-diagram/

Explore the processes that the product supports

Every internal product that has existed for a while supports at least one business process. When you go to explore those business processes, you'll discover the way the process is supposed to happen and the way it actually happens. Understand how the process works in the real world, because that's going to tell you how the rebuilt product should operate. Using collaborative modeling[39] to create a process model[40] is the best way to get to that understanding.

Play the risk management game

Just because you are rebuilding an existing system does not mean your effort is without risk. In fact, one of the reasons the product you are rebuilding is so old is because of all the risks that exist in rebuilding it. Use the risk management game[41] to identify, categorize, and determine how to address the key risks you face. And make sure you actually use the results of this exercise to guide your prioritization decisions. You'll be glad you did.

Map out your crappy first draft

Regardless of what some overzealous agile coach tells you, DO NOT jump immediately to brainstorming backlog items without first doing the activities mentioned above. Without the understanding those discussions bring, any effort at backlog creation is merely sticky note theater. When you do have the insights from those exercises, you'll have a good overview of the problem and possible solution so you can start synthesizing what you have learned and think about how you may go about breaking the work up into backlog items.[42] Story mapping[43] can help you plot

---

[39] https://www.kbp.media/collaborative-modeling/
[40] https://www.kbp.media/process-model/
[41] https://www.kbp.media/risk-management-game/
[42] https://www.kbp.media/story-mapping/
[43] https://www.kbp.media/story-mapping/

things out and think about how to group your backlog items in a meaningful way. It will at least help guide the conversation.

Implementing COTS or SaaS solutions

Most organizations do not develop 100% of the software that they use, nor should they.

A vast majority of the jobs they have to do can be satisfied with readily available COTS software, or its more modern successor, SaaS.

Why go through the pain of building something to address the same need that thousands of others have and that many developers have put in the effort to figure out already?

Yet, the organizations that primarily use software developed by someone else are the same ones that are now trying to become more agile, at least in their IT departments. Those folks look at the various frameworks for agile software development (primarily Scrum and SAFe) and say: "That's great if you're building software, but what if you primarily purchase and implement it instead?"

Here are some things you need to consider when implementing a COTS or SaaS solution in your organization.

Fall in love with the problem, not the solution

All too often, organizations implement COTS or SaaS products because someone with a great deal of influence or authority came across a "must-have tool" and began hunting for a reason to introduce it.

Far better to approach this from the opposite direction: start with the problem and describe that problem in terms of what value it has for the organization. I find that collaborating with impacted stakeholders to create a problem statement (see Chapter 8) can help you build a shared understanding of the problem.

When you understand the issue at hand and want to identify possible solutions (some of which may not require software), you may find a technique such as Impact Mapping[44] helpful.

Once you've identified desirable characteristics of your solution (hint: do not just look at the feature list of someone's pet product and crib off of that), describe those characteristics in the form of user stories or job stories so that you can focus on the problems you are trying to solve.

Pick the right solution

Now that you understand the problem and know what you'd like in a solution, you can decide whether it makes more sense to build or to buy. Using purpose based alignment can help you determine the right path. If your solution will differentiate you in your market, it probably needs to be unique, so building the solution is most likely the better choice.

If the solution is parity for your market, you may find that you can buy an existing solution. Should you go this route, resist the urge to customize whatever it is that you buy. That is a sure way to blow your budget and timeline and probably fail at achieving your desired outcome.

Instead, find the solution that is the most closely aligned with your desired characteristics, and revise processes or expectations in the small cases where you don't have alignment. This is a parity activity. There is no value in doing it uniquely.

Iterate and increment to learn

When most people think of applying agile to COTS or SaaS, they are trying to figure out how to fit the work of implementing the solution into sprints. There is certainly validity in figuring that out, but it's essential to understand why.

---

44 https://www.kbp.media/impact-mapping/

You don't iterate and increment for the sake of doing things in sprints. Rather, you iterate and increment in order to learn.

Most COTS and SaaS solutions require some amount of configuration, integration with existing systems, and the transformation and loading of data from a current system. These activities provide great opportunities for an iterative and incremental approach. The two primary ways you can approach it are:

Gradually roll out functionality. Start using the new solution for limited purposes. Perform the configuration and integration to support just that functionality, deploy it, and observe the results. Determine what you can learn from that rollout to apply to, configure, and deploy subsequent functionality.

Gradually roll out to new users. Have a small subset of the total planned user base start using the solution and closely watch the challenges they run into and the feedback they have. Use that feedback to alter your configuration and approach to roll out to the next set of users.

When you pick your first users, make sure you select people who are comfortable with change and adept at using products so that they can provide meaningful feedback.

You may find that in some situations you can combine both approaches, especially when different groups of users use different functionality. The key to picking the right approach is to select the one that will allow you to learn the most with the least amount of impact to ongoing operations as you make your transition.

If you must transition data or content from your existing solution to a new solution, do not wait until the last minute to do it. Find a way to transition it as soon as possible. If the data changes rapidly, you may have to wait until just before go-live. If it rarely changes, move it over immediately so you can test your new solution in as realistic a setting as possible.

Business intelligence

Business intelligence projects typically involve pulling data together from other products in order to help people in your organization answer questions or make decisions.

If you've worked in business intelligence for any length of time, then you've experienced the ongoing discovery that happens with business intelligence efforts. Once you get a feel for the kind of information that business intelligence can provide, you come up with all kinds of things you can use the data for that you didn't think of initially.

Here are some ways you can improve the effectiveness of your business intelligence efforts.

Express your outcomes as questions and decisions

Every initiative is more effective if you can describe success in terms of the outcomes you want to reach instead of the outputs you want to deliver.

With business intelligence initiatives, those outcomes are best described as questions you want to answer or decisions you want to make. When you describe outcomes in that way, you will experience the following benefits:

- You can deliver something quickly that provides your customers with value as you build out the rest of your data warehouse.
- When you go through a full pass of all the steps to deliver a data warehouse on a small subset of the overall data warehouse, you can learn things that can be applied to the rest of the data warehouse.
- You can focus on only the data you need and avoid using data that will not be used, saving analysis, development, and testing time.

- By organizing your work around specific outcomes, you can get a more useful indication of progress.

I've found that Socratic questioning is an effective way to uncover those questions and decisions.

You can capture these questions or decisions in the form of a user story (As a <who>, I want <what> so that <why>), a job story (When <situation>, I want to <motivation> so that <outcome>), or using other template of your choice. The format doesn't matter.

What does matter is that you identify distinct questions and decisions (outcomes) that are satisfied by big chunks of functionality you want to deliver (output). You can call the big chunks features, epics, or whatever term you prefer—again, it doesn't matter. I'll use the term "big chunk" for the rest of this section.

By organizing your work around each big chunk, you can deliver the functionality that delivers the data formatted in a way necessary to answer a question or make a decision. If you focus on one big chunk at a time, deliver it to your customers and then get feedback on that big chunk, you can use that feedback to revise your approach to subsequent big chunks. You may decide to deliver different big chunks, the same big chunks in a different order, or in another way altogether.

Whatever changes you make, you'll find that you more effectively deliver the functionality necessary to answer questions and make decisions, and you can avoid unnecessary work.

Incrementally deliver value

A common assumption about business intelligence is that you must get all the data warehouse functionality to its final form before it can provide any value. However, you may find that you can provide value in many ways before getting to the final desired form of data access.

Even though your user ultimately wants to get to a daily report with all the data they need, you may find you can manually extract specific data from the source systems and place it in a single table that your users can manually query to get the answers to their question.

Once you verify that you have the correct data, you can automate the process, organize the data in a more user-friendly manner and perform necessary transformations to the data as you extract it from the original source systems and provide it to your users.

In his book *Agile Data Warehousing*, Ralph Hughes provides a way to slice up the big chunks of business intelligence work into smaller improvements to the process as described above. There are a variety of characteristics of both the user-facing data view and the back-end data storage that you can gradually improve to achieve a level of functionality that provides the most value for your users.

Here are a few of Hughes' suggestions:

Data View (Front-End) Decomposition

- Refresh Frequency: How frequently is the user's data view updated?
- User Friendliness: How can the user access the data?
- Automation Level: What triggers a refresh of the data view?
- Transformation Type: What transformations (if any) happen between data storage and the data view?
- Data Storage (Back-End) Decomposition
- Refresh Frequency: How frequently is data from the original sources updated?

- Refresh Type: When a refresh from the original sources occurs, how is the data updated?
- Transformation Type: What transformations (if any) happen between the original sources and the data storage?
- Target Layer: What layers in the architecture are updated when a data refresh occurs?

The idea is to gradually improve on a specific characteristic one small chunk at a time. For example, you may start off with users manually querying directly against the data storage using SQL. You can then improve this experience with small chunks that introduce each of the following changes:

- Offer access through a controlled querying environment where links between tables are pre-built.
- Provide data in a report that the user can refresh manually.
- Automatically deliver the report to the user on a regular schedule.

After each step, get feedback from the users to determine if you have met their needs or if additional improvements are necessary.

IT Service Team

IT service work includes areas such as service desk, release management, and configuration management that are related to providing information technology services in an organization. There are several other areas that could be included in this description, and I could spark several semantic arguments about what is included in the IT service work category.

To keep things simple, I'm talking about those teams in an IT organization that tend to have work with the following characteristics (as opposed to teams that work on software development projects):

- Work items usually take the form of a request or a ticket. These items show up at unpredictable times.
- Some items are extremely time-sensitive, especially if they deal with people not being able to get their work done, while other items represent changes which are not as urgent.
- Each item is independent from every other item. This means that as soon as you finish the requested action you can deliver the results to the requester without waiting to finish other unrelated items.
- Items generally have less uncertainty surrounding them than items on a software development backlog might have. The only exception to this is when the item represents a bug that requires investigation to identify the root cause.

Work flows through an IT service team

You can group agile frameworks into two groups: those based on timeboxed iterations, such as Scrum, and those based on flow, such as Kanban.

Each type of framework is better suited for different situations. The context in which you want to apply each framework helps you determine which framework works better for your team to establish your methodology.

Flow frameworks are better suited to IT service work than timeboxed iterations, for a variety of reasons:

- Flow approaches provide greater flexibility to deal with priorities that change frequently. You can change your priority every time you start working on a new item.
- Flow approaches are better suited for work items that show up randomly, are independent of each other and are generally not part of a bigger whole.

- Flow approaches are better suited for work items that you can deliver when you finish rather than those that need to be grouped together with other changes.

To describe how to apply a flow approach to an IT service team, let's look at a team that maintains a not-for-profit professional organization's website, including membership administration, event registration, and community groups.

Work flows into this team when someone submits a question, request, or complaint via a form on the organization's website. The team can't know when these questions will come in, and the items vary in their urgency. The team also has a few ongoing efforts to introduce changes to the website driven by new programs or events.

The team has five members, each with their own area of responsibility. A few of the members can back up the others when necessary or deal with the more involved support situations.

The team is distributed, so they use an online dashboard (Trello) to keep track of the items they must work on and the items that are in progress. Because the items do not all have a consistent workflow, they keep their board straightforward by dividing items into the following sections:

- New: Newly identified items generated by the team or requested via a form on the website.
- On Deck: Items that have been triaged and have sufficient information to proceed.
- In Process: Items that a team member has picked up to work on.
- Waiting for Verification: Items that have been completed and are awaiting verification that the work was completed appropriately.
- Verified: Items verified by the requestor or another team member.

- Done: Items implemented on the website or requests delivered to the requestor.

When someone submits a request via a form on an organization's website, the form sends an email notification which Trello converts to a work item in the New section.

The team members take turns triaging the new items. As part of their triage activity, they determine the urgency of the item and classify the work (i.e., membership, event registration, or website content). The team member doing the triage sets the appropriate label. They then move the item On Deck and prioritize it in relation to other On Deck items.

When a team member moves an item they were working on from In Process to Waiting for Verification, they check the On Deck section for a new work item. The team has some rules that everyone uses to select an item based on priority and the type of work that each item represents.

The best of both approaches

Even though the team uses a flow approach, they've adopted some practices used by teams working in an iterative fashion, mainly because they found value in adopting those practices, not because anyone required them to.

A regular planning cadence

Every other week, the team gets together to look at the On Deck section and determine if the items are in the proper order, whether there are any new initiatives that they need to account for, and whether there are any items On Deck that could be removed altogether.

This discussion is like a sprint planning meeting with the exception that the resulting queue—in this case the On Deck section— is not set in stone. Essentially, this discussion serves to reorder the On Deck items based on the team's current understanding of priorities.

Daily stand-ups at the board

The team gets together daily to briefly discuss what everyone is doing that day and to determine if there any In Process items have hit a roadblock. During these stand-ups, the team members discuss:

- What the team needs to do to get things moved across the board.
- Based on what is known right now, what item the team should start working on next whenever there is room.

Retrospectives around the board

The team also finds value in a retrospective every other week to discuss how to improve their process. They have this retrospective while looking at the board, because it provides insight into how the team is doing. The questions the team asks during these retrospectives include:

- Is there any hidden work that's not represented on the board?
- Do we need to add a queue section?
- Are there any impediments? How can we remove them?
- Are we tracking things at the right level?

The team used these retrospectives to end up at their current process. They certainly didn't start using a flow approach with the process described here. Rather, that process evolved as the team got some experience and held retrospectives to gradually improve the process.

Measure and learn

To aid with their retrospective, the team tracks a small set of metrics that also help them identify obstacles in their process. These metrics include:

- Throughput (the number of items completed this week)
- Lead time for each item (completed date and start date)
- Average lead time for this week
- Items completed with > 0 blocked days
- Total blocked days
- A list of places where items were blocked

The team made a point of tracking their blockages because those blockages are good pointers to areas for improvement.

Your product is a big part of context

As you can see, the type of product you're working on influences what techniques you'll use and when. If you keep that in mind, you'll find yourself less frustrated when the data warehouse project you're working on doesn't quite seem to match that textbook description of a project you always read about.

Take some time at the beginning of a project to understand the nature of the product you're working on and figure out how you want to proceed.

And don't be afraid to adjust multiple times when you learn what you thought was true just ain't so.

Chapter 7 – Context: Consider Your Customers, Users, and Stakeholders

Another key part of context is the people you ~~have to~~ get to work with. Product development—whether it's products for sale or internal products—is ultimately an exercise in working with people.

To make it fun and interesting, those people have a wide variety of perspectives and have different relationships with the product. Those people are your customers, users, and stakeholders.

Customers

The customers of your organization are those whose needs you're trying to satisfy through building or updating the product. They give your organization money in exchange for some product or service.

For that product to appeal to those people, it should satisfy a need they have.

If the product you work on for your organization is the thing you're selling to your customers, the importance of understanding those needs should be fairly evident. But what if you work on a product that you don't sell but rather supports the actual products or services you provide your customer? What if you work on your organization's website, mobile app, claims processing application, HR system, or conference submission system?

Customer needs still matter.

Customer needs and digital products

If you work on a website, mobile app, or any other digital product that customers directly interact with, your product may not be the thing you sell, but it certainly helps you satisfy your customers' needs.

Understand your customers' needs to make sure you make the right changes to the website and to make sure you make the right design decisions for those changes.

Customer needs and enterprise products

If you work on a claims processing app, HR system, conference submission system, or some other enterprise product that your customers may not even know exists, customer needs are still relevant. You want to understand how your product supports the processes necessary for your organization can satisfy your customers' needs.

For example, let's say you work on a claims processing system for an insurance company. Your product supports a process that provides value to your customer. Your customers bought an insurance policy to manage their risk. They need the insurance policy to do its job—help them recover financially from an accident.

A customer-focused approach to processing claims means you'll make sure that the process results in the appropriate decision in the shortest time possible.

There is a balance. You won't approve those claims that clearly fall outside of coverage, because that will result in higher premiums or an inability to cover risks down the road, which does no one any good.

Focus first on the needs of your organization and you may find yourself inclined to skew the process in favor of your organization, to the detriment of your customers. This may benefit your organization in the short term, but in the long run it results in a loss of customers and potentially failure of the business.

Want to build the right thing? Focus on your organization's customers.

Understanding customer needs helps you make decisions about whether to update or replace an enterprise product and how you approach the changes you choose to make. If the process you are improving is a differentiating activity for your organization, you want to take a unique and creative approach to it. If the process is parity, mimic what already works in your industry.

Users

When it comes to determining if someone is a customer, user, or stakeholder, the users are the easiest to classify.

A user is anyone who uses your product. They may be inside or outside your organization. Ironically, in the case of internal products, users are often taken for granted. The line of thought is that users didn't really have a choice whether or not they used an internal product—it's their job—so why care about the experience they had?

People do have a choice. And they can be quite crafty in finding ways around using a product that is a pain to use. Or they use the product but they dread it, and that outlook results in mistakes.

What if internal products were built with as much thought to being delightful to use as products sold directly to consumers?

People might enjoy their jobs more. They might do a better job. They might treat their customers better. Everyone wins!

Okay, that may be a bit of a stretch.

But improved user experience is a vital aspect of building powerful internal products. It starts with understanding your users and using techniques to make sure you don't build something they dread using.

Stakeholders

Stakeholders are problematic.

Okay, perhaps I should say that differently. The concept of a stakeholder is problematic. (Although I know some of you immediately thought "You said it!" and had a particular person in mind.)

Technically, a stakeholder is anyone who impacts or is impacted by an organization's actions or products. By that definition, customers, users, and anyone inside your organization with an interest in your product is classified as a stakeholder.

That definition isn't very helpful if you're trying to differentiate between customers, users, and those internal folks who have an interest in your product.

Since saying "those internal folks who have an interest in your product" can quickly become cumbersome, I apply the term stakeholders to that group specifically.

Stakeholders play a big part in internal products. If you're not careful, you can easily confuse them for "internal" customers.

Don't do that.

Rich Mironov pointed out what happens when you confuse stakeholders for customers:

- Budgeting replaces prioritization—decisions about what to (or whether to) build for internal organizations are based on spending a budget (spend it or lose it) rather than considering priorities across all the possible activities.

- Scorekeeping is based on delivery dates rather than business outcomes—success is measured on whether something was delivered by an arbitrarily determined date rather than according to specific business objectives.
- Short term trade-offs accumulate over the long run—because it's intended for use inside the organization and we're very focused on delivery date, there is a large temptation to forgo good engineering practices (automated tests, usability, clearing up technical debt in appropriate places).

The road to bloated internal products is paved (using gold plating) with features added to appease stakeholders that do nothing for your organization's real customers.

It's easy to do. Stakeholders may control access to the users because the users work for the stakeholders.

Or the stakeholders are the users.

It can be very tempting to ask them what they want and just deliver that.

Except that isn't necessarily going to result in something that's good for your organization's actual customers.

You can't ignore your stakeholders, and you can't focus solely on them either. When your product is used by both stakeholders and customers, customer needs should trump those of your stakeholders.

Make things seamless for your customers, even if in the short term they may be a little clunky for your stakeholders.

But don't make it painful for your stakeholders. Remember you want to have a product that your users don't dread using.

Why it's important to understand these different perspectives

These differing perspectives play a part in your overall effort to introduce powerful internal products.

You determine the right thing to build in a broad sense based on what will satisfy customer needs. You may struggle to decide whether to favor what's best for your customers or best for your business, but it's not a matter of either/or, it's a matter of both. Do those things that are best for your customer *and* are good for your business.

You consider users when you make design decisions. You want to build your product so that people choose to use it if they have a choice, and look forward to using it if they don't have a choice.

Your stakeholders introduce considerations—in the form of constraints, risks, assumptions, and dependencies—into what you build.

Stakeholders may be directly involved in satisfying customer needs and look to your product to help them do that. If you're working on your organization's website or mobile app (now commonly lumped under the term "digital"), you're in this situation.

Stakeholders may work on internally focused business processes without interacting directly with your organization's customers. If you work on something like an HR or accounting system, you're in this situation.

Use the impact on actual customers to determine whether to undertake work for those stakeholders and the degree to which you perform that work. The purpose based alignment model is helpful here.

Once you've decided the extent of the product you're building, it may be helpful to view your stakeholders as users—if in fact they are.

The key point: you should understand the relationship people have with your product and the perspective they hold, and then work with them accordingly.

It does depend

It really does, unfortunately, depend. A lot of factors influence the techniques you use in any given project or any given product.

You need to understand your organization's strategy and structure, your product, and your customers, users, and stakeholders.

There are probably other factors as well. The key is to think about everything that could impact the techniques you use and take those things into account. That may not be the most satisfying answer, but it is a practice that will serve you well.

Chapter 8 – How to Deliver Maximum Outcome with Minimum Output

As discussed in Chapter 3, outcomes are changes in the world that happen because of your work. Outputs are the things you deliver in order to realize those outcomes.

It's easy to say "deliver maximum outcome with minimum output." It's another thing altogether to make that happen.

Here are the activities I've found helpful for realizing maximum outcome with minimum output:

- Identify the need to satisfy.
- Define success in a measurable fashion.
- Organize your roadmap based on the needs you're satisfying.

Identify the need to satisfy

When you start a new effort and are given a solution, it's easy to fall into the trap of just filling in the specifics. Unfortunately, things are not as clear-cut as they sometimes seem.

People tend to hang on to the first solution they think of when they face a problem and fail to question whether that first solution is the best. So when sponsors are asked to describe a request, they inevitably describe the first solution they envisioned.

One of your primary responsibilities as a business analyst is to dig into that solution and discover the underlying need. A simple approach I've found to accomplish this is to guide a conversation about a problem statement with the sponsor of the project and the team working on it.

Explicitly discuss the problem

I was working with a team in the midst of a commission system revision project. There were 11 people involved, including the sponsor, a couple of subject matter experts, and the majority of the delivery team. I wanted to get a better understanding of what the project was all about, and to find out if the team had a shared understanding of why they were doing the project.

I asked everyone to grab four index cards and a marker. Then I asked each of them to finish these phrases, one for each card:

The problem of... [Describe the problem] affects... [Who are the stakeholders affected by the problem]

the impact of which is... [What is the impact of the problem]

A successful solution would... [List the key characteristics that the solution, however implemented must have to be successful]

One set of cards looked like this:

> **The problem of:** completing the monthly commission process in a timely manner **affects:** agents, commissions staff **the impact of which is:** there is a delay for agents to get paid, commissions staff are constantly harassed by agents right at the time when they are the busiest (running the commissions process)

> **A successful solution would:** speed up the commission process, decrease the number of times agents bother commissions staff

The team member states a problem, but then identifies multiple stakeholders who are affected, multiple impacts, and multiple characteristics of a good solution. That's fine because you are primarily trying to generate information at this point.

Once everyone wrote their cards, I asked each team member to read their statements in order and place their cards on four parts of a table, each part corresponding to a section of the problem statement. If you are using sticky notes you can have people put the sticky notes on four separate sheets of paper hanging on a wall.

We ended up with 11 different perceptions of what the project was about, ranging from making some changes to the commission system, to making it easier to maintain, to completely overhauling how the organization paid its agents. Needless to say, the team was surprised by the different perspectives, considering that the project had been underway for a few months. Everyone just assumed that they were "all on the same page" until they did this exercise.

We had already gained value from the exercise because it exposed the disconnects in the group on the real need the project was trying to satisfy. We still needed to take the disparate items and condense them together into a single, consistent, agreed-upon statement. I had the group start at the problem cards and agree on a specific problem. Then, and only then, I had them move to the next the set of cards and repeat the process.

The result was a consistent statement they all agreed to and could refer to when they were trying to remember, or explain to someone else, what the project was all about. I didn't keep track of what the actual statement was—the more important outcome of the exercise was the shared understanding between the team members.

That said, the output from the exercise is useful. The stakeholders identified in the "affects" cards hint at whose needs you want to satisfy. The "impact" cards identify specific things you can look to eliminate, and the "characteristics of a successful solution" hint at potential acceptance criteria.

By working through the different portions of the problem statement, we converged on a shared understanding of the purpose of the project. Later, the team members were able to use this as one way of deciding where they should and shouldn't focus their efforts.

I did this exercise after the team had already started the project, because that's when I started working with them. Ideally, you'd like to have this conversation when the team is finding out about a new project. I've started a project with this conversation several times and found the teams are much better aligned on what they are trying to accomplish from the beginning.

The discussions that occur when formulating a consistent problem statement can also help the team focus. When your team crafts individual problem statements and then looks at all the pieces together you identify several different problems, stakeholders, impacts, and characteristics of a successful solution. As the team tries to arrive at one problem statement, their discussions raise issues, risks, and assumptions that may not have been apparent to everyone. Talking through those issues, risks, and assumptions helps your team build a shared understanding of the problem to solve and things they should consider when picking the appropriate solution.

Define success in a measurable fashion

How can you effectively determine if something is worth it? You need to understand what you mean when you ask that question. That means establishing clear objectives that you can use to measure success. You want to measure success in terms of the need satisfied (i.e., the outcome) instead of based on a specific solution (the output). This allows your organization to first determine if the need is worth satisfying at all, and then, if necessary, assess different solutions to determine which one is the most effective at satisfying the need. You may even find that even though the need is worth satisfying the cost of delivering any of the solutions outweighs the benefit gained from satisfying the need.

To reinforce the characteristics of good objectives, Tom Gilb in *Competitive Engineering* suggests a set of attributes which you can identify for each objective. Table 1 shows those attributes, with examples based on a website looking to increase the number of newsletter subscribers.

Table 2. Characteristics of good objectives.

Attribute	Description	Example
Name	Unique name for the objective	Increase number of subscribers per month within 6 months
Units	What to measure (*scale*)	The change in newsletter subscribers in a calendar month average
Method	How to measure (*meter*)	Subtract the number of subscribers at the end of previous month from the number of subscribers at the end of the current month, and average those changes over the months being measured
Target	Success level you're aiming to achieve	Average increase of 25 subscribers/month
Constraint	Failure level you're aiming to avoid	Average increase of 10 subscribers/month
Baseline	Current performance level	Average increase of 10 subscribers/month

A benefit of describing these attributes is the discussion that occurs in order to decide what the target and constraint should be, as it allows the team to get a clearer understanding of what success looks like.

Understanding the need first and being able to describe it via objectives gives you a chance to ask, "Is this need worth satisfying?" So in the example above, the team can ask:

- Is it worth it to increase the number of subscribers we add per month?
- Do we need to do things to just increase the number of new subscribers, or do we also need to worry about retaining existing subscribers?
- What is too much to spend trying to accomplish this?
- What are we forgoing by increasing the number of subscribers?

When setting objectives, be very careful about unintended consequences. The discussion above focuses on using objectives for the purpose of making decisions about projects or products and can drive behaviors in the teams working on those projects. This is especially true if those objectives are also used for the purposes of performance reviews. The financial services company referenced in Chapter 5 faced a significant scandal because employees created fake accounts in order to meet the sales objectives used to measure their performance. This is a dysfunctional use of objectives if there ever was one, and something you need to watch out for.

So what do you do if you are unable to come up with a meaningful measurable objective? Perhaps there is no clear measure of success for your situation. Perhaps there is a measure that you could use, but measuring it effectively is extremely difficult.

Perhaps establishing a baseline is politically undesirable.

I've worked on more than a few projects with the stated purpose of reducing manual processes. The real purpose is usually to reduce the likelihood and impact of human errors that could result in loss of money for the organization. Ideally, we would track the cost and frequency of errors before the changes and as a result of the revisions. But often these organizations don't officially measure those things and there is little energy for establishing that sort of measurement because of the political situation.

On one of these projects, we chose to use decision filters to at least make the team consider whether it was reasonable to expect that changes we were making would reduce manual processes, and as a result reduce the possibility and cost of errors. It was not perfect, but we at least had something to base decisions on.

Use outcomes to decide what to do and what not to do

Even if your organization makes decisions about whether or not to pursue a project with a defined timeframe, budget, and scope, there is still value in approaching those decisions through an outcome lens.

Frame the decision around whether you should make an investment in order to satisfy a particular need. The trick is getting all the people involved with that decision to build a shared understanding about what that need is and decide that it should be solved within certain constraints (for how much and by when) rather than making an explicit decision about how that need is satisfied.

That is, I realize, easier said than done.

Structure your projects around outcomes

Most organizations that make investment decisions with a project paradigm tend to decide whether or not to do a specific project. That means they are deciding whether to implement a specific solution.

That type of decision making results in project decisions framed like these examples:

- Rewrite a 20-year-old client server app that supports a crucial business process.
- Bring customers for a given product line on the same ordering system that three other product lines are on.
- Introduce an express pickup service.

On the surface, these all appear to be good projects, and it should be easy to tell when each is done. Right?

Maybe not.

Sure, you could claim that the rewrite is done when the new product is up and running. But does that mean you have to recreate all of the functionality on the existing system, even if something isn't relevant after 20 years?

You know you're done moving customers over to a new ordering system when they are on the new ordering system. (Yes, that is a bit tautological.) But do you know for sure that moving the customers to the new ordering system is going to accomplish what you set out to do? Do you know what you set out to do?

Let me rephrase that. Do you know why you wanted to move customers over to a new ordering system?

You know you're done introducing a new express pickup service when people can use it. But again, how do you know that service was a success?

To know when those projects were successful, you need to know the need each project was trying to solve. You need to know why it's worth doing that project.

You need to understand the outcome.

The best way I've found to drive projects with an outcome focus is to have a discussion with the person or people who are proposing the project, key stakeholders who are impacted by the investment, and the people who ultimately decide whether or not to do the project.

I gather those people in a room and write 10 questions on a whiteboard, leaving plenty of space between each question to write notes and answers.

The questions I like to use come from my variation of Marty Cagan's opportunity assessment,[45] and guide the discussion around reasons to consider the investment:

Exactly what need will this satisfy? This question may be difficult to answer, but it's very important to get it right so that you can ensure that you are trying to satisfy a clearly defined need and don't just have a solution in search of a problem.

For whom do we satisfy that need? This question seeks to identify the key stakeholders and the people who will have a vested interest in the product.

What can be gained from satisfying this need? This question identifies the benefits to be gained from the product. Don't feel as if you need a precise answer at this point. An order-of-magnitude answer is usually good enough to determine whether the need is worth satisfying.

How will we measure success? This is a way of identifying outcome based metrics[46] relevant to the product.

---

[45] https://www.kbp.media/internal-product-opportunity-assessment/
[46] https://www.kbp.media/outcome-based-metrics/

What alternatives are out there now? This is another way of asking what would happen if you don't satisfy this need, as well as identifying different ways of satisfying it.

Do we have the right people to satisfy this need? This question is about whether you have the appropriate skill sets on the team, and if not, whether you need to bring in help from inside or outside the organization.

Why now? This question asks what time constraints, if any, exist for delivering the product.

How will we encourage adoption? This is to get you thinking about change management and implementation.

What factors are critical to success?

This singles out any specific requirements identified during the discussion or subsequent analysis. This question is not meant to identify the solution; rather, it highlights any dependencies or constraints that may exist.

Is this need worth satisfying? This question sums up the discussion. Based on what you've discussed up to this point, is this project worth it?

Start with the first question and don't move to the next until you agree on the need—or if you identified more than one, on which of those needs is most important.

That need will drive the answers to the remaining questions, so it's important to settle on one.

You may run into a situation where you get about halfway through and the group's understanding of the need changes. If you need to circle back and clarify, do that.

If you structure your discussion this way and get to the last question, you'll no doubt get some push back that "we can't decide whether it's worth it without knowing how much it will cost."

If that happens, reframe the question. Instead of trying to figure out how much it's going to cost to fix—you can't know that with any reasonable accuracy at the point when you should be having this discussion—ask everyone how much they'd be willing to spend to satisfy the need.

It's a subtle difference, but an important one. You're providing a constraint that may actually lead to a more innovative solution.

Make outcome informed decisions

I've had experience with projects very similar to these. I had the opportunity to lead an organization through a discussion laid out this way to discuss introducing a service similar to the express pickup service. By talking through the 10 questions, we discovered that there wasn't a clear understanding of the need the project sponsor was trying to address.

Once the group determined the need they were trying to satisfy, they realized the originally identified solution would not have addressed that need. The organization avoided a great deal of work and was able to focus on other efforts that were addressing clear needs.

This is the power of outcome informed decisions. Avoid doing unnecessary work before you even start.

Use outcomes to decide how to deliver a solution

I know most of you are rarely involved in discussions that early. I can hear you now: "That's great Kent, but I'm never in that situation! What do I do when I get told to deliver something?"

Fair enough. You can still use outcomes, but instead of using them to decide whether to start a project, use them to decide how to deliver the project.

Establish your outcome

Usually, when you're asked to deliver something, that ask tends to be fairly specific. It's usually in the form of a solution to deliver, such as the three previous examples:

- Rewrite a 20-year-old client server app that supports a crucial business process.
- Bring customers for a given product line on the same ordering system that three other product lines are on.
- Introduce an express pickup service.

Each of these describes a solution: an output. What you want to know is why the person requesting the investments wants **these** outputs. You want to know what outcome they are looking for— why you're doing the rewrite, or switching the order system for a specific customer, or introducing an express pickup service.

You want to know what problem you're trying to solve.

You could use the opportunity assessment described above, but the results may be disappointing when you find out that you aren't in a position to not do that particular initiative. Explicitly asking if a problem is worth solving when you've already been told to solve it might be frowned upon.

So when I'm working on a project the organization has already decided to do, I find it's better to use an exercise that helps build shared understanding around the outcome. I like to use a problem statement.[47]

I gather the team, the project sponsor, and any key stakeholders for a discussion. As you might imagine, these types of discussions can be difficult to schedule because the sponsor and some of the stakeholders may have several competing priorities and busy schedules. Be firm. Have this discussion as close to the

---

[47] https://www.kbp.media/problem-statement/

start of the project and don't hold the discussion unless the key players are there.

It helps to explain why you're having the discussion and inviting the people you're inviting. Let everyone know that you're trying to build shared understanding about the intent of the project. You're not questioning the project, you're making sure everyone understands it the same way. This hopefully encourages the sponsor and stakeholders to make time in their schedule.

If you find that some of the key players are not making time, you can always consider the nuclear option. Ask the sponsor and stakeholders if they can't set aside an hour for a discussion to make sure a project delivers on its intent, how important is that project? (Consider the impact on your job and influence in the organization before you exercise this option.)

Once you have everyone together, ask the project sponsor to explain what the investment is intended to accomplish. They will generally describe it in output terms at this point, which is fine.

Give everyone a chance to ask questions to clarify what the sponsor said. Don't be surprised if there aren't many questions. People probably will not fully understand but also will not be willing to speak up.

Next, ask everyone to take four sticky notes and write the following:

- The problem of <Describe the problem>
- Affects <Who are the stakeholders affected by the problem?>
- The impact of which is <What is the impact of the problem?>
- A successful solution would <List the critical benefits or key capabilities that the solution—however implemented—must have to be successful>

Once everyone has written their cards, ask participants to read their statements in order and place their cards on four parts of the wall—each part corresponding to a part of the problem statement.

You may have fairly consistent descriptions of the problem or widely varying descriptions. I've found that the variation depends on how long the team has been working on an investment before this type of level setting. The longer the team has worked without level setting, the more variance there will be.

After everyone has read their statements, have the group work through each part of the problem statement and come up with a statement that they can all support.

This discussion will lead to an overarching problem statement for your work and a better understanding of a variety of key aspects.

Agreement around the first point (*the problem of*) brings clear agreement around the problem you're trying to solve. This may also help you understand your main decision filter.[48]

Agreement around the second point (*affects*) identifies the people that are experiencing the problem. These are people you want to make sure you're considering and you go through the work of resolving the problem.

Agreement around the third point (*the impact of which is*) helps you understand why it's a problem and why it's worth solving. And yes, if it becomes clear during the discussion that the problem is not worth solving, explore that with your sponsor. You may discover that the problem is worth solving with a smaller investment than what's planned. Better to determine that early on then making a large investment on a small problem.

---

[48] https://www.kbp.media/decisionfilters/

Agreement around the fourth point (*A successful solution would*) helps you to identify any constraints you need to work under and may also point out a couple more decision filters.

You now have a view of the problem you're trying to solve that you can use to guide decisions moving forward.

You have your decision filters.

You have defined scope in terms of an outcome rather than a list of outputs.

You are now in a position to make outcome influenced decisions to ensure an effective investment. The nature of those decisions varies based on the type of investment you're making. Let's look at some variations based on the examples described above.

Rewrite only what you need to reach your outcome

System rewrites have gotten a bad rap (somewhat justified) because they often become an exercise in dressing up clunky processes, bad rules, and jumbled up data in a shiny new technology wrapper.

Teams are handed an unreasonable deadline and an insufficient budget and asked to rebuild a system. The expectation, whether stated or not, is that the new system will do everything that the old system did.

Scope is described in terms of all the functionality you have to rebuild in the new product.

Except you probably shouldn't replace all the functionality that exists in the current system. Some of that functionality is no longer needed. You may take this opportunity to revise the process.

Don't define scope based on a list of outputs you think you need to deliver. Define your scope based on the outcome you intend to deliver. A definition of scope based on outcome allows you to operate in time and cost constraints and still flex within the output you deliver, as long as you satisfy the desired outcome.

I've previously described how a team I worked with used discovery sessions to build an initial understanding of an investment to rebuild an existing internal product.[49] The purpose of that activity was to understand the problem, the environment, and how the new solution could address the problem without recreating all the necessary functionality.

We used the results of those discovery sessions, continued discovery along the way, and constantly reflected on our decision filters to make sure we produced only the outputs we needed and to build those outputs in a sequence that helped us learn what other outputs were needed.

Does this solution bring the results you want?

When you want to add more products to an existing ordering system or introduce a new express pickup service you may not be worried as much about the scope as you are about whether that's the right solution to your problem.

The way you define scope is not as big a concern as understanding whether the identified solution solves the problem you're setting out to solve, or if there is a simpler, less expensive way.

In this case, you want to be clear with your decision filters and then explore different ways to accomplish that outcome, which may be significantly different than changing the ordering system they use.

This is a good situation to use impact mapping[50] or other techniques to make sure you're solving the right problem. Look for ways to shorten the feedback cycle so you can try something, see how it works, and identify if it's the solution you're looking

---

[49] https://www.kbp.media/initial-discovery-new-internal-product/
[50] https://www.kbp.media/impact-mapping/

for. You may find that the solution you end up delivering is quite different than the one originally identified.

Decide how to deliver an outcome

At the end of the day, just because you've been handed a solution doesn't mean that you still can't figure out what outcome people are expecting and find a way to deliver that outcome in the most effective way possible. It may just be in a different way than the folks who approved the investment originally thought.

Organize your roadmap based on the needs you're satisfying

I often help product owners get a better handle on what product ownership is, especially how it relates to their organization. One question I usually receive during those discussions is, What must a product owner include on their product roadmap?

It's important to understand what someone means when they say "product roadmap." The person who asked me the question was looking for some way to convey the expected timeframe of specific deliveries for projects she does for clients. In other words, a roadmap as SAFe describes it.[51]

Most product people would say that's not really a product roadmap, or at least not a very good one, because it doesn't take uncertainty into account. Yes, the SAFe version of a roadmap indicates a "commitment" and a "forecast." It also shows dates and specific features, so it implies more certainty than is probably realistic. Stakeholders outside of the team like this type of roadmap because it tells them when things will be delivered ... until things aren't delivered on those dates.

---

[51] http://www.scaledagileframework.com/roadmap/

A better way to think of a product roadmap is as a statement of intent for how you are going to implement your strategy. The product roadmap is a living thing that indicates your best understanding at the point that you last updated, and it reflects whatever uncertainty you faced when you last put it together.

What to include on a roadmap

With that in mind, the things you should include on the product roadmap include:

- Different time horizons
- Outcomes rather than outputs
- Ties back to strategy

Here's an example of what a roadmap including those things might look like.

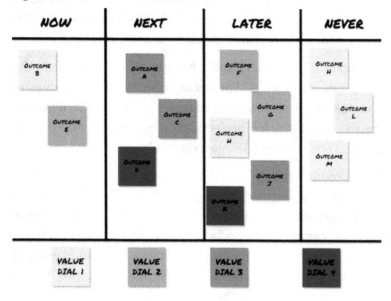

Figure 12. *Example of a simple but effective product roadmap using sticky notes.*

Different time horizons

Use time horizons that reflect increasing uncertainty. Instead of dates, I use Now, Next, and Future.

- Now – outcomes you know you're working to deliver now or will start working on soon.
- Next – outcomes you think you'll work on soon, with the understanding that things could change.
- Future – outcomes you might tackle sometime. Those are the most likely to change as time proceeds.

Don't use dates, because when you update the roadmap you don't know when things are going to get done. If there are real-time constraints driving the need to work on a specific outcome, you may want to note that.

Outcomes rather than outputs

Describe the needs you want to satisfy rather than the solution you're going to use to satisfy that need. For the items in Now, you probably have a solution in mind but there's no guarantee that will be the solution you ultimately use. Using this approach, you're properly setting expectations that you're going to solve a specific problem—you just don't know exactly how.

I will admit it's tough to do this all the time, and I find myself occasionally listing a specific feature the team is going to deliver or an action I'm going to take. It's probably okay once in a while in the Now column, but not a good idea in Next or Future.

Ties back to strategy

Depending on your work, this could be your organization's strategy or your product strategy. In the case of the Agile Alliance, I organize the outcomes listed in each horizon under the "Value Dial" that outcome impacts. You can think of the value dials as the way that the Agile Alliance describes its strategy in order to make decisions about what to do and what not to do.

This is also a good place to invoke the decision filters which are based on strategy. When you examine an item on the roadmap, ask "Will this help us achieve [some item from strategy]?" If it does not, remove the item from the roadmap.

You may not always need a roadmap like this

Chapter 6 explained that an important piece of context is the type of product you're working on. One place where that context makes a difference is what a product roadmap for that type of product would look like, or even whether one is necessary.

For internal products, you may use a roadmap of the type described above for your overall project portfolio. It provides guidance as to which outcomes you're trying to deliver in a given timeframe, and the specific solution approach may result in digital transformation activities, back office work, implementing a COTS system, or business intelligence.

Once you've determined the nature of your solution, you may produce something that looks like a roadmap but is better described as a delivery plan, as it will no doubt be more feature based and show what will be delivered in each quarter.

Having a product roadmap for support does not make sense, as this type of product is inherently reactive.

You may have something which resembles a roadmap for maintenance activity, but it won't be a true roadmap. What you'd most likely see is a plan for which maintenance activities you're planning to do in each month or quarter.

How to make the roadmap a living thing

Whether you have a roadmap as described above or something more like a delivery plan, revisit it on a regular basis. Update it to reflect the things you've done, the things you've learned, and the changes in your organization and environment. This helps to keep the roadmap fresh and useful.

I revised the product roadmap for the Agile Alliance website about every three months as a way to update the Board of Directors. I found that was a good cycle to revisit what we did and adjust our thoughts about what things were coming next.

In other cases you may revise your roadmap much more frequently, usually when you uncover some new information that influences where things fit on the roadmap.

CHAPTER 9 – HOW TO BUILD AND MAINTAIN SHARED UNDERSTANDING

Shared understanding answers two questions: Does your team understand the need you're trying to satisfy, and do you all agree about the characteristics a solution should have? The people who should have that shared understanding are those who have the need (usually customers, sponsors, and stakeholders) and those who deliver the solution (the team).

The act of building a shared understanding in a collaborative fashion is just as important as the resulting shared understanding itself. The conversations that occur while building shared understanding give your team a clearer picture of the problems customers and stakeholders face, and identify risks and assumptions that are relevant to an effective solution.

The approach I use to build and maintain a shared understanding may look backward when you compare it to how you'd typically go about building your actual product. I tend to start with the outcome I'm trying to deliver and determine what I need to deliver that outcome. This order is based on an approach with an obscure name, but a powerful message—feature injection. I'll explain it a bit more below.

As a product person you hold the vision of the outcome, and you should guide the discussion to make sure the feature your team arrives at satisfies that outcome. You also bring an understanding of the business-related constraints (primarily time and cost) to the discussion.

You need the perspectives of your customers, stakeholders, and users in order to provide insight on their desired outcome and the context to identify what will make a solution valuable.

You need the perspectives of your team and their understanding of the available technology to identify solutions that are feasible and usable.

When you build shared understanding you start with a desired outcome and arrive at the right set of user stories through design thinking,[52] analysis, and conversations.

This description assumes that you have identified features that you believe will help your customers achieve their desired outcome and that you have determined that a particular feature is the next best thing to work on.

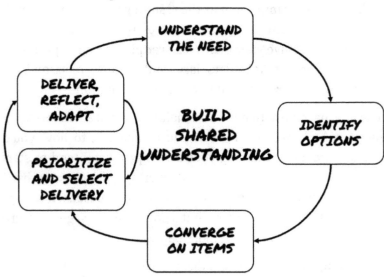

Figure 13. Building shared understanding requires an ongoing cycle of activities.

---

[52] https://www.kbp.media/portfolio/design-thinking/

Building shared understanding is not a scheduled meeting. It's an ongoing activity. Some parts may be done as a specific event, and others occur throughout the course of working on a product. You may find yourself doing some things on an ongoing basis, but different steps in the cycle are more prevalent at certain times than others.

You'll find that you generally cycle through the following activities to build a shared understanding. I describe these activities in more detail later in this chapter.

- Understand the need
- Identify options

Converge on items

Then you'll get into a smaller cycle within the larger one, where you iterate between these steps:

- Prioritize and select delivery
- Deliver, reflect, and adapt

During those iterations you will probably identify new options for delivering the feature based on feedback and remove some of the items you had identified before. That's natural, expected, and a good thing.

Once you deliver a feature that properly satisfies the desired outcome, you then circle back to identify a new outcome and a new feature and start the whole cycle over again.

The techniques you use during these activities are the same business analysis techniques you've spent your career perfecting. The difference is you use these techniques to build a shared understanding rather than produce requirements.

Don't view requirements as your ultimate deliverable; see them as a means to the end of building a shared understanding. Everyone on your team knows what need you're trying to satisfy and the solution you're building to satisfy it.

What you're really doing is managing risk—primarily the risk that the team forgets about key stakeholders or overlooks some important data or process relevant to the solution. Keep your team informed about important data and processes. Communicate that information in an easy to consume way. Help your team maintain their pace, and you will improve your chances of satisfying your customer's needs.

Feature injection – from outcome to output to process to input

Feature injection is a helpful approach to analysis, created by Chris Matts, that's not explicitly used as much as it probably should be.

Feature injection is based on identifying the value an initiative intends to deliver (its outcome), delivering the features that provide that value, and building a shared understanding about those features, primarily through examples.

Identify the value

Feature injection begins by creating understanding about the business value an initiative is trying to deliver (in other words, why are we doing it in the first place). In a for-profit organization, an initiative delivers business value when it increases or protects revenue or reduces or avoids cost in alignment with organizational strategy. In a more general sense, I like to gauge the business value of an initiative based on whether it helps an organization meet one or more of its objectives.

For example, let's say you are working at a health insurance company facing the prospect of an increased claim volume, but the leaders of the claim area would prefer to not add staff too soon. One area they feel would help them process more claims with the same staff is in the claims intake—they still receive a considerable number of paper claims which have to be entered in the claim processing system. With that in mind, the health insurance company establishes an objective: Reduce the number of paper claims received from 1,000 per week to 500 per week within six months.

Once you understand the objective you can identify a solution you think will meet that objective, and then identify the assumptions underlying your belief that the chosen solution is the right one.

To continue our health insurance example:

Building and hosting a website where single-provider offices can submit their claims will help us reduce our paper claims.

Assumptions:

- Most of our paper claims come from single-provider offices.
- Most single-provider offices have internet access.
- Most single-provider offices do not have medical billing systems.
- If we build a website, our single-provider offices will use it.

Inject the features

Once you understand the value you are trying to deliver and the assumptions that impact that value, you can use that information to guide what you do next. You want to select chunks of your solution that either allow you to make progress toward the targeted objectives or help you validate assumptions.

For the sake of continuity, I'm going to refer to those chunks of a solution as features—it is called feature injection, after all. However, I feel compelled to address some key points about the use of the word "feature," as it is used in several different ways.

Have a shared understanding of what "feature" means to you and your team. The BABOK Guide v3 defines a feature as "a distinguishing characteristic of a solution that implements a cohesive set of requirements and which delivers value for a set of stakeholders."

I define features in this book as something your product has or is—this is typically functionality offered by your product that enables users to do something. That definition is inspired by a Dan Schewan article ("Features vs. Benefits"[53]) that has a more prominent marketing slant. I like this definition better because it ties in with outcome based thinking. In fact, that's how Schewan describes benefits: "the outcomes or results that users will (hopefully) experience by using your product or service."

Agree to how you represent features in your backlog. Just as it's important to agree what you mean when you say "feature," it's also helpful to agree to how you will represent that concept in your backlog.

Some teams are driven to have features as backlog items because they are using SAFe. That's partly because SAFe has a complicated requirements hierarchy of three or more levels. I'm not a fan of a backlog hierarchy greater than two levels.

There is value to having different levels of granularity in your product backlog. It allows you to easily change priorities on work that you have not started yet, and it allows you to incorporate what you learn in how you structure your product backlog. Your product backlog will be a lot more manageable, and you'll avoid rework.

You generally want two granularities in your product backlog:

- **Big chunks that represent things your stakeholders, users, or customers want to**

---

[53] https://www.wordstream.com/blog/ws/2017/02/21/features-vs-benefits

accomplish. These are your epics. Use these epics to do higher level prioritization and indicate progress to your stakeholders using a technique such as the parking lot diagram.

- **Small chunks that represent the smaller aspects of the solution that your team will implement.** These are your user stories. Each user story should still add some new capability and provide a means for your team to get some feedback. These user stories provide the team a mechanism to plan out their specific work and a way to organize their detailed description of the product.

That's all you need. If there are additional levels in your hierarchy, any benefit (which, frankly, I've never experienced) is overridden by the work of maintaining those extra levels and the soul-draining conversations you'll end up having over whether something is level A or level B.

But what about if we split an epic and find that some of the user stories are still too big to fit into a sprint? Split those user stories into smaller user stories. It's okay. The world will not end.

I also find it's best to keep the concept of features out of the backlog. Backlog items describe changes to your product in order to reach an outcome. Features describe something your product has or is.

I choose to use the concept of epics in my backlogs to represent what needs to happen in order to realize features.

Epics are for customers; user stories are for the team. Although it was not the original intent of the user story, in practice, user stories have become small, granular pieces of the overall output that often need to be combined with a few others to help customers, stakeholders, and users achieve their desired outcome. Items initially placed on a backlog based on discussions with customers tie directly to a particular outcome and are often called an epic. They are then broken down into user stories to help the team organize their work in an incremental and iterative fashion.

With those three ideas in mind, think of an epic as an output that you think will help your customer achieve an outcome. User stories are small granular items that your team may deliver in order to deliver the broader feature and ultimately help your customers achieve their desired outcome.

Which aspect you focus on first will depend on how far along you are in the initiative. At the start, you will most likely spend more effort on validating assumptions (you can also think of this as reducing uncertainty) and follow up with delivering features that you know will deliver the value you seek.

This is where analysis techniques and the idea of working from output to input come into play, especially those representing displays of information or reports that help stakeholders answer questions or make decisions, or which support a broader process.

Once you understand the outputs, you can work backward to figure out what processes are needed to produce those outputs (including the rules that act on those processes) and the inputs needed to create the outputs. You are effectively performing analysis in the opposite direction of development, which tends to bring in the inputs of a system first, then build the process, and finally create the outputs.

Said another way: because you are pulling value from the system via the outputs, you leave a hole at the beginning of the system into which features are injected. That's how the name feature injection is derived—as we pull business value from the system, we inject the features that create that value.

For our health insurance example, the team would probably first attempt to validate the key assumptions mentioned above. If those assumptions prove correct, the team can then model the online claims system (rough wireframes should be sufficient) and start iteratively building the system, collecting feedback at frequent increments throughout the process.

The key point here is that you identify value first, then iteratively identify the features that you need to deliver it. Don't brainstorm a big list of possible changes and try to figure out what each feature could contribute to business value. Focus only on those features that directly lead to satisfying your objective.

Spot the examples

We typically use models to describe the outputs and processes and the inputs used to create them. These models are helpful for creating shared understanding with everyone involved in delivering the features, but they are rarely sufficient. One way to improve the overall understanding of a model is to add examples. Examples serve two purposes: First, they provide concrete guidance in very specific situations to people who tend to ask, "Yes, but what about this situation?" And second, examples give the team a way to test the models and make sure they account for different situations that may occur.

The thought process surrounding feature injection is a huge influence on how I approach product work, and while I very rarely mention the name to the teams I'm working with, I'll often introduce the ideas. Most of the people I talk to say things like, "Yes, that makes a lot of sense. Why didn't we do that before?" or, "Yeah, we do that, with these few tweaks."

Starting with the value you want to deliver, using that value to decide what feature to deliver next, and describing that feature through the use of real-life examples is a simple, effective way to build the right thing and not build things that aren't necessary.

Understand the need

You need to keep the team and your stakeholders focused on why you are working on the product. This is certainly important when you're starting a project. It's equally important to do when you're in the midst of a project, especially if you change teams, your team changes, or other conditions change.

You choose to add or revise a feature on your product because you believe it will have an impact for your customer. It may not help them fully reach the outcome they desire, but it should certainly get them closer.

Make sure that your team understands what that desired outcome is going to be and agrees that it's possible to make that happen. You can usually accomplish that by discussing the metric you're going to use to gauge the success of the feature as you deliver it. In some cases, it's difficult to find a concrete measurement that tells you whether you've satisfied your customers' needs. You may need to find some qualitative ways to determine that.

Starting work on a project

When you start a project, use the problem statement exercise (described in Chapter 8) or some other technique to make sure you understand the real need you are trying to satisfy and how you'll know when you've met it. Take the output of that exercise and post it where everyone can see it. Then, when you find yourself involved in the inevitable discussion (argument) about whether some feature should be included or how to go about doing it, point to the problem statement and ask, "Will what we're talking about help us do that?" Decision filters can provide the same type of guiding star.

When you create a backlog, don't just dive in and brainstorm a bunch of things to do. Instead, start with your outcome—the need you are trying to satisfy—and then identify what specific things will position you best to reach that outcome. That's the practical application of feature injection.

When you don't know what the solution should look like

When you don't know what output is needed, you may find impact mapping[54] helpful. Impact mapping structures conversations around four key questions:

- **Why are we doing this?** The answer to this question is the goal that the project is trying to accomplish as measured by an objective.
- **Who can bring the organization closer to this objective, or conversely, who may prevent us from reaching the objective?** The answer to this question identifies the actors who can have some impact on the outcome.
- **How should our actors' behavior change?** The answers generate the impacts you're trying to create.
- **What can the organization (specifically the delivery team) do to support the desired impacts?** The answer to this question identifies the deliverables, which will typically be software features and organizational activities.

---

[54] https://www.kbp.media/impact-mapping/

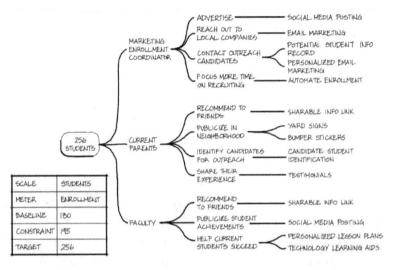

Figure 14. An impact map for a project to increase student enrollment.

In other words, impact mapping helps you identify a solution based on which solution will drive the customer behavior changes that will help you realize a specific outcome.

To identify a solution with impact mapping:

1. Get the team and stakeholders together.
2. Identify the objective (why).
3. Think about people whose behavior can help the organization get closer to the goal, or people whose behavior will move the organization farther away from the goal (actors— who).
4. For all the actors you identified, think about what behaviors you want them to start or change to help your organization get closer to the objective, or behaviors you want them to stop because they are preventing your organization from getting closer to those objectives (impacts).

5. For each behavior, identify things that the organization can deliver to drive changes in those behaviors (deliverables).
6. Decide which deliverable to deliver first and gauge its impact on the targeted objective.

When you have an idea of your solution

When you do have a clearer idea of what your solution should be, such as when you're replacing an existing internal product, you can use story mapping to manage your ideas.

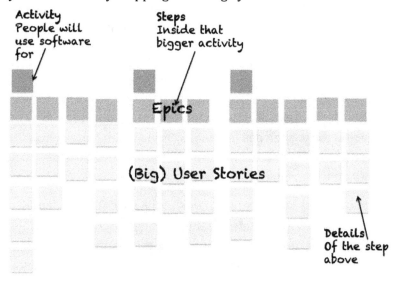

Figure 15. A story map illustrates how a project's activities are broken into epics and user stories.

When you use story mapping, you identify the main activities that your users perform, the steps inside those broader activities, and then details or different ways to support those steps.

This adds some context to your backlog and provides a tool you can use to detail implementation order.

Even if you are working on a solution that does not have a large amount of user interaction and does not clearly support a business process, the story map format can still help you understand the context of your backlog.

Frame the problem. Establish a shared understanding of the need the solution is intended to satisfy.

Map the big picture. Lay out the story map using features as the high-level items across the top of the map. If you have different types of users who can use specific types of features, it may help to organize the features by user. If there are any obvious user stories, place them under the appropriate feature at this point.

Explore. Select the feature(s) you believe you will be delivering first and do a deep dive on them via conversation with the interested stakeholders. Sketch models to aid the conversation. (You may find those sketches helpful later when you start delivering those particular stories.) As you have those discussions, you may refine your map.

Slice out a release strategy. Look at the user stories identified for the features and determine the minimum user stories needed to deliver the desired goal. The idea is to identify the minimum output to deliver the maximum outcome. Organize these user stories into a set of releases by moving them vertically.

Identify the first items. Once you have identified a set of releases, you may find it helpful to identify the user stories you want to start with, as experiments to validate key assumptions or reduce risk. These stories become the topics of your first iteration.

During a project

If you are in the midst of a project and you sense that the team does not all share the same understanding of the need you are trying to satisfy, or if you realize that you are actually trying to satisfy a need, I suggest that you stop for an hour and create a problem statement, described in Chapter 8. The goal is not necessarily the problem statement itself, but the conversation that comes with it.

Remember that other members of the team are focused on other aspects of the product:

- How will we build it? (developers)
- What happens in this case? (testers)

While they all may have the reason for doing the project in the back of their heads (and the good ones can hold multiple concerns front of mind at the same time) they are also probably subconsciously counting on you to keep an eye on those things.

AgileAlliance.org search

Throughout this chapter, I'll use the example of revising the search functionality on agilealliance.org to demonstrate how I go about building shared understanding. The outcomes we sought to influence were to: Make information on AgileAlliance.org easier to find in order to *improve brand awareness* and *increase value to members*. Those items are two of Agile Alliance's value dials, which you can think of as organizational decision filters.

The team got together at the beginning of 2017 and discussed the issues we experienced with the search results. We also talked about the resource displays in general and how the content was organized on the site. The content was organized based on resource type—video, event session, book, blog post—instead of by topic. We determined—based on feedback we received and by examining other, similar sites—that organizing content by topic was a more intuitive route.

During the discussion we reasoned that combining the listing of resources and search results would address several of the issues on the site. We called the resulting feature Search Filter Order. Not the sexiest name, but we all understood what it meant.

Once we determined a general direction, we supplemented our discussion with a whiteboard sketch which gave us something to point to and reference.

We determined that one of the things we could do to impact these dials was to improve the search capabilities of the site—primarily by making the search results more relevant, but also by making the user experience of the search results more intuitive.

In the case of search on AgileAlliance.org, we thought that improving the search functionality would improve brand awareness and increase value to members. We reasoned that people would be able to find information on a specific topic quicker, thus making the site a more useful resource.

There are no metrics that we could look at to gauge whether our search result changes had a direct impact on those value dials, so we looked at the general trends in website traffic and specific behavior surrounding the search results pages to give us an indication of how the feature performed.

Identify options

Using the collaborative model as a guide, identify all the things you could possibly do as part of that feature. You want to use *divergent thinking*, so try to keep the constraints fairly flexible (although, to provide a little focus, keep the overall outcome in mind).

These options can be alternative approaches, and can also be the things that need to occur in order to make the feature happen. Once you've identified the general direction of the feature, it can be very helpful to have your model on a whiteboard and identify all the things you could do to deliver it on sticky notes. Where possible, place those ideas on the appropriate part of the model to provide some context.

The options you identify are candidates for user stories, but you may find that some end up being a bit too big and will need to be split, which you will start doing in the next step.

You may find story mapping helpful to identify options, especially if you are working on a full customer journey or trying to support a process.

AgileAlliance.org search

With AgileAlliance.org search, the sketch of the result page was on a whiteboard and we used sticky notes to record every aspect of the search capability. Sadly, we didn't take any pictures of the whiteboard in that state, although it looked like an office supply store blew up in the room.

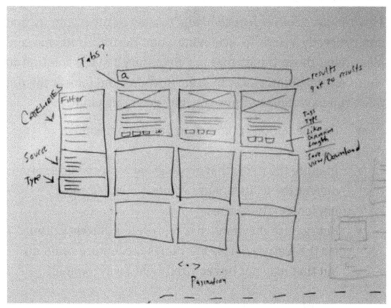

Figure 16. A sketch of the intended search result page for a website update project.

The notes included a variety of things we wanted to do with search, many of which were influenced by what we had sketched on the whiteboard, such as the ability to filter results by a variety of attributes, the ability to change the order of the displayed results, the ability to like and save certain items, and pagination for the display.

At this point, the sky was the limit, *as long as* the item was relevant to helping people search for a specific resource on AgileAlliance.org.

Converge on items

Get a general agreement with respect to the output that will get you there. When you identify the backlog items you need in order to deliver a feature, you are starting to have discussions in earnest about your chosen solution. This is where collaborative modeling using mockups and process flows is very effective.

This requires *convergent thinking:* tossing out the options that don't directly relate to achieving your desired outcome and identifying those things that are necessary for the solution to work. At this point, you stop brainstorming and look at the options you have. Some things you may do at this point:

- Cut the options that exceed one of your known constraints.
- Identify the items that are missing and are necessary to deliver the feature, such as infrastructure and implementation items.
- Reorganize the items that represent different options for the feature. These are things the feature could do but that may not be required right away, or at all.

Some techniques that you may find helpful for this discussion are example mapping[55] and story splitting.[56] These techniques are typically used when you are refining backlog items, but the structure and some of the ideas contained in these approaches can also be helpful when you identify backlog items to realize a feature. Both techniques put the team in the right frame of mind for identifying the small implementation chunks that add some sort of value to your customer. You may not get the items down to a size that fits in an iteration, but you can at least get them into chunks that allow you to consider which ones you want to deliver in which order.

AgileAlliance.org search

For search on AgileAlliance.org, we threw out some things such as liking content or saving content to a dashboard, because we knew those items were beyond what we wanted to accomplish with this feature.

The team identified some infrastructure work, such as selecting an indexing mechanism, and the work necessary to integrate the new search functionality into WordPress. The team also included backlog items for the transition work to replace the existing resource listings with the newly built search results listings, which would serve double duty as a resource listing.

To help us choose which options we could implement and to give us some items to work with when selecting our first delivery, we split the broad concepts such as filtering into smaller items. The resulting user stories that we derived from "filter" were:

- Filter results by type (event session, post, video, etc.)

---

55 https://www.kbp.media/portfolio/example-mapping/
56
https://www.kbp.media/?download_id=89b0c6cece99ea453c8327794dd13df8

- Filter results by topic (people, process, technology)
- Filter results by event (a specific conference)
- Filter results by initiative (Technical Debt, Agile Accounting, Manifesto Translation, etc.)
- Admin can select Taxonomies and their values to allow users to filter by (categories, tags)

These items represent different attributes that the results could have. Your domain likely has similar domain-specific terms. When you use them, make sure everyone on the team agrees what they mean. The team did have a shared understanding of what these terms mean in our context, so they acted as good placeholders. As it turned out, most of these items were of the appropriate size and were not split down any further, but they could have been as the team started digging into a particular item.

Prioritize and select delivery

You can get a lot of value out of having big items on your backlog (i.e., epics) because you can get a broad view of the overall output you might need to deliver without having to dive into detail on any one item too soon.

At some point though, you do need to dive into detail on something in order to start delivery. Backlog refinement lets you do that in a way that allows you consider options and focus on the essential aspects of the feature, discarding the aspects that aren't completely necessary.

Once you have a collection of items that your team feels adequately covers what you want to deliver with your feature, you then need to identify the subset of the items you want to deliver first (or next).

At this point, you have an interesting decision to make regarding prioritization. You could say that you'd like the team to size all of the items related to that feature to help you prioritize, or you may decide to do an initial prioritization to indicate which items you'd like to have the team size first. It all comes down to what type of decisions you need to make and what information you feel you need to make those decisions.

You'll generally find that you have a certain set of items you know you have to do in order to have a usable feature. Other items may provide some value if you add them, but that value may not outweigh the cost of delivering them.

You also need to decide whether to deliver in order to learn (an MVP approach[57]) or deliver in order to earn (an MMF approach[58]). The approach you choose dictates to some extent the items you include in the first delivery.

Whatever you choose, make sure you can have the quickest feedback cycle possible, so you are positioned to deliver something, get feedback, and adjust, which is the next step.

For more information see "Is there a difference between MVP and MMF"[59] on KBP.media.

AgileAlliance.org search

When we were worked on search for AgileAlliance.org, I prioritized the items and put them into three groups—A, B, and C—based on Todd Little's approach to prioritizing backlogs:

- **Group A:** MUST be completed in order to ship the product. You will change schedule if necessary to make this commitment.
- **Group B:** WISHED to be completed in order to ship the product, but may be dropped without consequence.

---

[57] https://www.agilealliance.org/glossary/mvp
[58] https://www.agilealliance.org/glossary/mmf/
[59] https://www.kbp.media/difference-mvp-mmf/

- **Group C:** NOT TARGETED to be completed before shipping, but might make it if time allows.

Group A included the infrastructure items and implementation items as well as base functionality that was necessary or search would be pointless.

Group B included some of the variations on filtering, as well as "nice to haves" in the result displays.

Group C included everything else that made the valuable, usable, and feasible cut.

The team started by sizing items in Groups A and B, and some of the Group C items if they had time. I mainly needed that information to determine how much we could get done within the allocated budget and whether I needed to ask for more budget in order to produce specific capabilities.

As the stories were sized, it became apparent that we'd have some tough decisions to make. The Search Filter Order addressed resource grid and search issues, but a lot had to happen in order to make it work. That meant we wouldn't be able to deliver everything I'd originally put into Group A at our current budget.

I printed out all the items so I could sort things and see what groupings would work. I took the approach of scaling back our expected outcome. I placed the Group A items that were needed to replace search functionality in one group (you can think of it as A1), and the items needed to display resources and search results in the same way as a separate group (A2).

Organizing the items this way was beneficial in a couple of ways. First, I was able to identify the items that should be included in the first delivery regardless of whether we got additional budget. That was the A1 group. Second, I was able to put together a cohesive feature with the A2 items that allowed me to guess at a size and identify a discernable value from those items.

Deliver, reflect, and adapt

At this point, you have a set of items that you can feed into your team's normal discovery and delivery process. The items may be properly sized user stories already, or you may need to split of them down even further.

You'll also describe the user stories and build the resulting functionality, delivering to your customers, stakeholders, or users once you have a valuable and usable set of functionality.

Gather feedback on the delivery and use that feedback to determine what aspects of the feature you release next.

Along the way, some of your "deliveries" may be internal to your team if you are trying to figure out some technical items, or they may be MVP-type work that you use to answer some questions or verify some assumptions.

At each delivery, have an honest, frank discussion around whether you've delivered the promise of the feature and whether you need to keep going or if you are truly done.

If you think you still need to deliver more items for the feature or the feedback tells you as much, you'll revisit the previous step to determine what you should work on next.

If you think you are done, you'll select a new outcome to deliver and circle back to the first step.

Describing user stories

People often ask how to use user stories to properly document requirements for a product, or whether they can or should be used that way.

Some people reading this will nod in agreement: "Yes, I've often wondered that myself." Others will cringe.

User stories weren't intended to be requirements. As Jeff Patton remembers it (retold in *User Story Mapping: Discover the Whole Story, Build the Right Product*), Kent Beck originally came up with the idea for user stories and described it this way:

> If we get together and talk about the problem we're solving with software, who'll use it, and why, then together we can arrive at a solution, and build shared understanding along the way.

User stories were intended as a means of providing some structure to conversation, to act as placeholders if you will. The aim of that conversation is to make sure everyone working on a product has a shared understanding of the product and what outcomes it's intended to produce.

They weren't intended as a documentation vehicle. But your team often needs a documentation vehicle to remember the specifics about your solution. I've started referring to those as backlog items and will do so throughout this book. If you prefer to call them user stories, feel free.

I find conversations with my team about what we need to build are invaluable. I also find that hand-waving, sketching, pointing, and moving cards around during those conversations helps us get to shared understanding much quicker.

Backlog items help you organize work and conversations. Models,[60] acceptance criteria,[61] and examples[62] help us make sure we're all on the same page during the conversation, and help us remember afterward what we talked about so we can go build it.

Don't rely on backlog items themselves to describe what you're building. They're the outline. The description comes in the form of the models, acceptance criteria, and examples you create during those conversations and keep around while building the product.

---

[60] https://www.kbp.media/collaborative-modeling/
[61] https://www.kbp.media/acceptance-criteria/
[62] https://www.kbp.media/examples/

You may use some tool to track your product backlog. The backlog items in that tool are items that you use for planning discussions. For the items that you're about ready to deliver, you have a conversation, record relevant acceptance criteria and examples in that item, and link out to relevant models. It's helpful to keep that information grouped together in the context of that story, although you'll find that some information is helpful to the group in the context of the broader product.

Afterwards, some of that information may be incorporated into system documentation[63] if it will help with future updates to the product. Some of it will be thrown away because it is no longer relevant given the new context of the product.

So instead of asking, how we can use user stories to document our requirements, perhaps a better question is, How can we build and maintain shared understanding of our product and its intended outcomes?

AgileAlliance.org search

The main question we had at AgileAlliance.org was what search mechanism that we were going to use. We weren't happy with the results that the built in WordPress search functionality gave us, so we explored the other available options to pick one that suited our needs—primarily the ability to influence relevancy with some rules. A key rule is relevancy based on the type of resource. For example, if you searched AgileAlliance.org for "backlog grooming" the first result we'd expect to come back is the backlog grooming glossary item. (Yes, I know "grooming" is not the favored word anymore, but many people still look for it in using that term. The glossary item does make the point that it is more properly called "backlog refinement.")

---

[63] https://www.kbp.media/system-documentation/

The team did some research on various search indexing mechanisms and then piloted a couple of them. We didn't release this functionality in the wild because the main question we were trying to answer was whether we could influence the relevancy of the results.

Once we selected our desired search indexing mechanism, we started working on the items to build out the search capabilities (Group A1). By this time, we were also able to secure some additional budget so we could also complete the display resources (Group A2) and search results items.

As we progressed, we were fortunate enough to discover some efficiencies that allowed us to get rid of some items that were addressed via work in previous items. That allowed us to build some additional features. Along the way, I reviewed the functionality built to date and provided the team feedback that they incorporated in their subsequent work.

Once we felt we had a usable solution that provided a bit of value, we started implementing it on the site. We switched the sitewide search over to the new search solution, and slowly started replacing our current resource display with the new functionality. Along the way the team continued adding functionality, which by this time included some capabilities that were not essential to the solution but did provide added value.

We were quite pleased with the end result, and all indications are that it has improved visitors' and members' ability to find resources on AgileAlliance.org.

In case you haven't had a chance to use the site search, here's what it looks like.

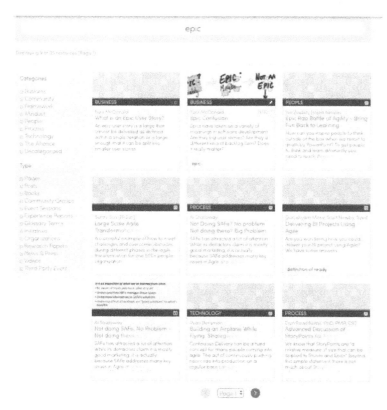

Figure 17. A screenshot from the completed AgileAlliance.org search function, showing the results for the word "epic."

If you remember nothing else

The important things to remember about building shared understanding are:

- Features give you a broad view of your solution and help you to determine where to focus each specific deep dive.
- Building shared understanding is a team sport.
- Building shared understanding starts with an outcome and arrives at the right set of user stories through design thinking, analysis, and conversations.
- Building shared understanding is an ongoing activity.

CHAPTER 10 – HOW TO MAKE SURE DECISIONS GET MADE

Once you have a shared understanding of what you're trying to accomplish, the next thing to do is provide guardrails for the decisions that team members make. While the leaders of an organization make key decisions, such as whether or not to create or update a product, the members of the team make many decisions on a day-to-day basis that impact the product. In order to make sure the team makes effective decisions, they need to keep those decisions in line with their shared understanding of the need the product is satisfying.

Common activities aligned with this habit include prioritizing which aspects of the need to satisfy (global) and prioritizing which aspects of the solution to deliver (local).

When you're the product person on the team you make sure that decisions get made—it's what you do. These range from broad decisions about the entire product down to day-to-day decisions on very specific design aspects of your product. You don't make all of those decisions yourself, but you certainly play a role in making sure that whoever does make the decisions does so in a timely and informed manner.

There's more to decision making than simply flipping a coin and calling heads and tails. As I reflect on the successful and not so successful decisions I've made, I've found the following aspects important to consider:

- What decisions
- Who decides
- When to decide

- How to decide
- Evaluating your decisions

This chapter explores each of these aspects at a broad level.

What decisions

Jeff Gothelf and Josh Seiden noted in Sense and Respond, "For information workers, thinking and decision making *are* the work."[64]

I had the opportunity to take part in the creation of version 2 of the Agile Extension to the Business Analysis Body of Knowledge. This was a great opportunity to shape the broader conversation on the intersection of agile and business analysis.

One of the things that I'm particularly pleased about in the Agile Extension is that we (Steve Adolph, Shane Hastie, James King, Ryland Leyton, Jas Phul, Paul Stapleton, Stephanie Vineyard and I) were able to explain how business analysis is involved in making a variety of decisions at three different horizons. It's important to understand these decisions because business analysis is often required to compile the information necessary to make these decisions.

The concept of horizons is not a uniquely agile idea, nor is it unique to business analysis. All product people have to make sure these decisions get made. The iterative nature of agile approaches with short feedback cycles makes it especially important to introduce this concept in order for efforts to be effective. It's also important to describe these decisions from a business analysis perspective to reinforce the role that business analysis plays in making these decisions.

Each horizon typically requires different decisions, and I've found different techniques helpful in addressing those decisions. (Thanks to Kupe Kupersmith, who contributed to this exploration.)

---

[64] http://amzn.to/2sjHVmw

Strategy horizon

The strategy horizon is where you consider the needs of your customers in relation to your organization's strategy to determine what initiatives you do and do not do. At least, in theory that's what is supposed to happen.

Some organizations don't really consider their customer's needs when they determine what IT initiatives to undertake.

Some organizations don't have an actionable strategy that helps them make decisions.

Some organizations don't decide what they won't do. (As important a decision as deciding what they will do).

There are two primary decisions about every idea at the strategy horizon. These decisions are generally made by product managers in an externally focused product setting and by someone with portfolio management responsibility in an internally focused situation.

Is it worth it?

You're really trying to decide if you have a need worth satisfying. In order to make that kind of decision you should know:

- The actual need (not just a symptom).
- The impact on your organization's customers. In other words, are you directly addressing a customer need or are you addressing the need of a stakeholder inside your organization that will impact your customers?
- Whether the benefit experienced from satisfying the need outweighs the cost of satisfying it. In some cases, this calculation will be very easy. In other cases, you may have to go with gut feel.

If you don't know the actual need, are not sure about the impact, and don't see a significant benefit, you should stop working on that idea.

If you determine that the need is worth satisfying, you then proceed to decide how to go about satisfying it, which plays into the next decision.

Helpful techniques

You can use a technique such as the opportunity assessment,[65] discussed in Chapter 8 to guide a conversation with key stakeholders in order to acquire the above information. You may also use a problem statement,[66] also discussed in Chapter 8, to answer the first question in the opportunity assessment so that you can more effectively home in on the actual need.

How is a business analyst involved?

As a business analyst, you often find yourself suggesting that these discussions should occur. You may also be the one who facilitates the discussion. You may find yourself shepherding the idea through the decision-making process to make sure there is an explicit decision made about whether the need is really worth satisfying.

Create, change, or pass

When your organization determines whether a need is worth satisfying, you then need to decide if you *are* going to satisfy it, how you'll organize the work, and what impact that might have on other initiatives already in progress.

Your organization's decision comes down to three possible approaches:

Create a new project to satisfy the need

This means that your organization needs to identify a team (or teams) who will work on that need and figure out where those teams are coming from. This last part is important and often

---

[65] https://www.kbp.media/internal-product-opportunity-assessment/
[66] https://www.kbp.media/problem-statement/

overlooked. If your organization decides to create the new initiative, you also need to determine how you will free people up to allow them to focus on it (as opposed to just adding the new initiative to an already overflowing backlog).

Change an existing project to satisfy the need

Your organization may choose to change the parameters of an existing project to meet the new need. The upside to this approach is that you don't have to identify a new team to focus on that need. The downside is that the original focus of the existing project may get lost.

Stop trying to satisfy the need

The need may be worth satisfying when examined in isolation, but it may not make sense when considered in the grand scheme of what your organization has going on. Or maybe you can't have a team work on that need at the moment without harming the progress of another equally important project.

Helpful techniques

A technique that can be helpful for assessing what teams currently have on their plates and which ones may have capacity is the portfolio alignment wall.[67] This is a way of viewing your organization's portfolio of active projects and the plans for a certain time period into the future. The results of the opportunity assessment, as well as the current capacity of all your teams, will help you determine which route to go with this decision.

An effective portfolio alignment wall provides transparency surrounding what different teams are working and provides a guide to conversations about dependencies and activities of the various teams.

67
https://www.stickyminds.com/sites/default/files/magazine/file/2012/360 4399.pdf

Start by gathering a representative or two from each team around a whiteboard that you don't mind dedicating to the portfolio alignment wall for a long period of time. If your teams are remote you can always use an electronic solution such as Trello.

Divide the whiteboard into a set of columns representing time periods such as a week or month, depending on how quick your feedback cycles are. If your teams organize work into sprints, you may have a column for each sprint.

When you create rows, you need to think about how your teams are organized. If you're doing a portfolio alignment wall for several teams that are all working on the same product, the rows can be major value streams of the product. If you have teams working on several different projects, then create a row for each team.

Since we're talking about a portfolio of projects, let's have each row represent a specific team. You may also want to note which product(s) a given team is responsible for, assuming they have a specific area of responsibility.

Then start using colored sticky notes to represent the various projects those teams are working on. If projects always stay inside the bounds of a single team, you can assign them all the same colored notes. If there may be more than one team working on a given project, you'll probably want to use a different color or shape of note for each project.

Put a sticky note in each column that you're planning on a team working on during a given project. If a team is working on more than one project in any given time period, put a sticky note for every project that the team has during that time period.

Continue until all the known projects are represented. You'll also want to create sticky notes for all the projects that your organization wants to do but has not assigned to a team yet. If you have some idea of when those projects may happen, create a row for unassigned projects and put a sticky note in each of the relevant time periods. In this case it's also helpful to note which products are impacted by that project.

At this point, some things will probably become apparent. You may notice that some (or all) teams have multiple sticky notes in each column, and you'll probably also note several sticky notes in the unassigned row. You may want to take a picture of the board at this point as a representation of the current state.

Now the tough conversations start.

Ask the group what would it look like if every team only had one sticky note in each cell. Which sticky notes would be removed or moved? Are there any projects that need to be done by a certain date versus others that have some time flexibility? Are there projects in the unassigned row that are more critical than the projects that are already in flight? Should those be switched?

Identify what you would like the workload for each team to be if there could be only one sticky note per team per time period. Note the questions and further investigations that need to occur to get to that state of affairs. The portfolio alignment wall is most effective when the people who are in a position to make the relevant decisions are involved in the discussion or are accessible to bring to the board to discuss.

Try to get teams focused on just one project per time period for the next three time periods. Then, reconvene the group at the portfolio alignment wall on a regular basis to discuss upcoming work, always trying to keep each team working on only one project.

The portfolio alignment wall won't necessarily give you all the answers, but it certainly will provide a backdrop for informed conversations and will make the situation painfully clear.

How is a business analyst involved?

As a business analyst, you typically elicit and organize information to support this decision. It's likely that if you shepherd consideration of the need, you have the best understanding of the need and how it fits with the skills and experience of the various teams in your organization.

Initiative horizon

Decisions in the initiative horizon focus on what solution your team uses to satisfy the need and whether it's worth proceeding once you select that solution.

Notice that your team doesn't decide on the solution until the initiative horizon because the team responsible for implementing the solution needs to be involved in that decision. You want the people who understand the capabilities of the available technology to be the ones who determine the best way to apply that technology.

The ownership of decisions in this horizon is a bit fuzzier, and different people may own different decisions. Ideally you'll have a person identified (usually a sponsor, product manager, or product owner) who has the primary decision responsibility for the initiative. That person should defer some of the decisions to the more technically experienced members of the team, or at least lean heavily on their input when making decisions. The best course of action is to discuss as a team who will make each of these decisions when you start any new work on your product.

What solution will satisfy the need?

In some cases, your team will know the outcome you're trying to reach but won't have a clear idea of the best way to satisfy those needs. In those cases, this decision is very relevant.

In other situations, your team will have a clear idea of the problem and the solution, in which case this decision may already be made for you. If you find yourself in this situation, make sure you confirm that the solution really is clear and is truly the best one. It doesn't hurt to take a quick step back to make sure you have a clear understanding of the need and have some definitive evidence that the solution you're going to implement is the correct one.

Helpful techniques

A useful technique for identifying potential solutions in a way that keeps your focus on the problem you're trying to solve is impact mapping[68] as described in Chapter 9. Impact mapping helps you structure a conversation by starting with the outcome you seek (stated as a measurable objective) and working from that to identify the people who can impact that outcome, the behaviors you need to change to drive that impact, and the things you can deliver to change those behaviors and experience that impact. John Cutler has suggested five questions[69] that can be helpful when trying to identify and assess the assumptions that are the basis of those solutions:

- Whose behavior will change because of this work?
- What is their current behavior?
- How will their behavior change?
- How will the new behavior pattern benefit the user?
- How will the new behavior pattern benefit the business?

How is a business analyst involved?

As a business analyst, you typically ensure that there is a clear outcome identified, preferably tied to a measurable objective, and facilitate discussions with the team to identify potential solutions. You'll also organize the information that results from that conversation and drive toward a decision on the preferred approach.

---

[68] https://www.kbp.media/impact-mapping/
[69] https://medium.com/%40johnpcutler/4-simple-questions-to-drive-validated-learning-548a51a70ee5

The most effective way to do that is to facilitate a discussion using a technique such as impact mapping and drive toward a decision.

Build vs. buy

Once your team has some insight into your preferred solution, you need to decide if you're going to build it in-house or buy it. If the choice is to buy a solution, you need to make sure you're selecting something that does not need a great deal of customization, or that you're willing to adjust your processes such that you don't need to customize your purchased tool a great deal.

If you can't find a tool that meets your needs, and you're unwilling to change your processes to match the available solutions, then you should probably consider the build option if the nature of the activity warrants it.

Helpful techniques

The purpose based alignment model described in Chapter 4 is a helpful tool for making this decision.

Once you understand the activities your product supports through the lens of purpose based alignment, you can decide the best way to approach delivering a solution.

Chances are your project delivers a solution that supports a parity activity or closes a parity gap. The typical design guidance for that situation is to achieve and maintain parity, simplify, and mimic.

Assuming a viable solution exists that supports accepted practices for that activity, you may be better off buying an existing solution. This is when purchasing a COTS or SaaS solution makes sense. If you do go down this path make sure you don't waste all advantage by customizing that solution. The more customization you do to the purchased solution, the more likely that you are treating your parity activity as if it were differentiating.

If you find that most of the available solutions partially support your current process, you may consider changing your process to match that of others in your market. An overly unique parity process that does not offer a competitive advantage is not the sign of a differentiating activity, it's a sign that you've made the parity activity too complicated.

For example, there's no need to roll your own timekeeping system. Chances are you can find an existing solution that will sufficiently meet your needs, even though you may need to simplify your process a little bit.

On the other hand, when you work on a solution that supports your organization's differentiating activity it makes complete sense to build that solution in-house. Differentiating activities require unique and innovative solutions.

If you follow the appropriate approach for dealing with parity activities, you'll be able to free yourself up to apply more innovation and creativity to the differentiating activities that warrant that design approach.

How is a business analyst involved?

As a business analyst, you typically elicit and organize information to support this decision. The most effective way to accomplish that by facilitating a discussion using the purpose based alignment model to identify the activities that you're supporting with this initiative, as well as what quadrant they fit in.

Choosing which aspect of the solution (epic) to deliver and when

Whether your team chooses to purchase a solution or build it in-house, you'll still want to slice that solution into smaller bits to provide short feedback cycles. For the sake of simplicity, I'm going to use the term "epic" to refer to the placeholders for those smaller solution components, as that is the term frequently used to refer to large items on a product backlog. While the term has a different meaning depending on which framework you use, I'm going with the originally intended definition in software development—a big user story.

With that in mind, this decision comes down to deciding which epics you need to deliver and in what order. What you're effectively doing here is stocking your backlog.

Helpful techniques

There are a variety of techniques such as process modeling and story mapping that can help you identify the epics you need to start with.

Process modeling

If your project supports a business process, you can often use a process model[70] to build out your backlog and identify the order of the items you deliver.

First, you need to model your process. I find the best way to do this is to get a group of subject matter experts and your team around a whiteboard and map the process out with sticky notes as the steps and decision points.

You want to be able to build the model as you discuss things and change the model as you work through the process and uncover information you didn't know at first. You will change things, and that's okay. It's the act of talking through the process that helps people build an understanding and think of things that they didn't realize when they started.

Here are the steps I usually like to follow when mapping a process:

Name your process. If you're working with an existing process, identify all the various ways the process is referred to and use a consistent name going forward. If you are creating a new

---

70 https://www.kbp.media/process-model/

process, create a name and consistently use that name. The clearest process names start with a verb (for example Submit Session Proposal or Adjudicate Claim). The more specific and action-oriented the name, the easier it is to keep people focused on the proper scope.

Determine whether you need to model both current state and future state, or just future state. When you change an existing process, start with the current state. Model how it currently works in reality, not how people think it should work or how it's written up in procedures and work instructions. Those differences between expectations and reality can help you to identify opportunities for improvement.

If it's a brand-new process, you may not have a current state to map. Either way, having the explicit discussion about whether you are modeling current state or future state helps to create clarity.

Identify a clear start point and end point for the process. Explicit starting and ending points help you keep the scope of your discussions contained. Identify what must be true in order for the process to start (pre conditions) and what conditions need to be in place to consider a process successfully completed (post conditions). You may also want to determine if there are certain activities that trigger the start of a process.

Choose the most common path through the process and identify the actions and decisions that occur. Select a scenario relevant to the process and talk through that scenario with the group, identifying the key actions and decisions along the way. For your first scenario, select something that is both common and fairly simple. This ensures you capture the key activities of the process and provides a structure to build on when you start discussing less common edge cases.

During this discussion you will most likely need to keep the group focused on the specific scenario you are discussing. If people bring up different scenarios, note them somewhere so that you can come back to them but stay focused on the desired flow. Whenever possible, find an actual example you can use to walk through the process.

Walk different scenarios through the process and adjust the process accordingly. Once you've walked through the most common scenario, identify other scenarios to walk through the process and adjust the process model based on those new scenarios. Usually, different scenarios drive new decision points or additional paths off existing decisions. Repeat this step for the different scenarios your team has identified.

Identify examples to test (and potentially break) the model. Select a couple of examples to walk through the process. These examples may represent one of the scenarios you already identified or slight variations. The goal here is to test how robust the model is for dealing with real-life scenarios and identifying gaps or assumptions that may exist in your process. If you identify an issue with your process model, revise accordingly.

Capture your process model with a picture. When your discussion is at a stopping point, take pictures of your process model and distribute them to the group. If possible, leave the actual model on the whiteboard so that you can have future discussions and revisit it if new information requires you to revise the model. If people were not able to join the discussion, review the process model with them (preferably in person at the whiteboard, but at least using the pictures). These discussions may reveal new information that drives revisions to your process model.

You can use the process model you created to provide a "big picture" view of your initiative and identify backlog items needed to support the process. This exercise can be done at the same time you model the process or shortly thereafter, depending on how much time you have available.

If you do end up having the discussion later, try to gather the same group of people together.

Identify backlog items. Provide the group with sticky notes, preferably in a different color than those used to create the process model. Ask the group to identify backlog items needed in order to make the process a reality. In some cases, the backlog item is directly associated with a particular activity in the process, in which case you can use the same phrase to describe both. In other situations, a backlog item may be a particular path through the process in order to support a given scenario—describe those backlog items in terms of the relevant scenario. Have people place the sticky notes on the appropriate location on the process model. This places the backlog items in the bigger context.

Review the backlog items. Once your team has identified potential backlog items, ask them to walk the model and see if anything is missing or if they have questions on anything. Have the appropriate discussions and add any missing backlog items.

Identify the backlog items that help you reach a specific outcome. Identify a specific outcome that you want to accomplish, most likely an interim step to your overall outcome. Have the team identify the specific backlog items that are absolutely essential to arriving at that outcome with a colored dot or a specifically colored marker. This step allows you to focus on only the backlog items that are essential to accomplishing your desired outcome.

A good criteria for your initial pass at identifying backlog items may be only those items required to support the most common scenario you had in mind when first modeling the process. If you have a specific set of outcomes that you would like to deliver incrementally, repeat this step for each outcome.

Story mapping

If your project deals with several user interactions with your project that cannot be consolidated into a single process flow, you may find story mapping[71] is a better way to identify backlog items and determine which ones to do first. Chapter 9 explains how.

How is a business analyst involved?

As a business analyst, you typically elicit and organize information to support this decision. If you are fulfilling the product owner role, you are responsible for making the decision regarding what epics to deliver and their order.

Continue, change, or cancel the project

This decision is one your team should make (or revisit, depending on how you look at it) multiple times through the course of the project. That's because you need to make sure you're incorporating new information that comes in from your delivery activities, as well as factoring in what's going on with other projects in your organization and the impacts of projects on each other.

Ultimately, this is a priority decision. What does your organization want its focus to be, and where do you want to apply your teams?

In practice this decision is not nearly as clear-cut as it should be. Organizations try to split the difference and avoid the hard "change or cancel" decisions by having teams focus on multiple projects. In this situation they have still made a choice, and it's not one they intended: none of the projects will make satisfactory progress.

---

[71] https://www.kbp.media/story-mapping/

Helpful techniques

To ensure that you have the proper information to make this decision, establish an outcome based metric+link++link+[72] and review its value after every change you make. Chapter 8 describes how to use outcome based metrics to decide what projects to start. Here's how you can use outcome based metrics on an ongoing basis to decide whether you should continue to work on a project.

Select an output, deliver that output, give it enough time to have some effect, and then compare the current value of the metric with your target and constraint. Did you reach your target? Then you can stop working on that particular outcome and move to something else.

Did you make progress toward the target, but didn't reach it? Identify the next possible solution you could try in addition to the one you just delivered.

Did you hit the constraint level? Back out the solution you just tried and try something else, or stop work on the effort.

How is a business analyst involved?

As a business analyst, you typically elicit and organize information to support this decision. You're also going to find yourself recommending a decision to the ultimate decision maker for the initiative.

Delivery horizon

Decisions in the delivery horizon focus on those decisions your team needs to make in order to build and deliver the selected solution.

The responsibility for making the decisions in this horizon varies depend on the specific decisions and may fall to a product

---

[72] https://www.kbp.media/outcome-based-metrics/

owner, a technical expert on your team, or you in a business analyst role.

What aspects of the solution to deliver and in what order

This is the primary decision made by your team (generally by the product owner) on a repeated basis during backlog refinement. You're determining which user stories are in, which are out, and in what order they'll be delivered.

Helpful techniques

A variety of techniques can help you determine which user stories should be delivered and in what order. You can refine the epics[73] you identified to determine potential user stories, then you can use story splitting[74] to further analyze those stories. See the discussion in Chapter 9 to understand how these techniques fit together to help you determine the order in which to deliver backlog items.

You may also find it helpful to track your entire backlog refinement process using a discovery board.[75]

Discovery boards are ways for teams to visualize their backlog refinement process. The best discovery boards consist of a whiteboard or wall divided into columns that reflect the steps a team takes to get product backlog items ready to be delivered (developed and tested) in an iteration. The backlog items are represented by sticky notes or cards that move across the board as the team builds a better understanding of the specifics of each story.

---

[73] https://www.kbp.media/feature-refinement/
[74] https://www.kbp.media/why-split-user-stories/
[75] https://www.kbp.media/discovery-board/

Once you've created your discovery board, use it as an ongoing reference point for the status of product backlog items in backlog refinement (the discovery process).

Depending on what columns are on the board, certain columns can be used as agendas for team events such as sizing discussions, and can even provide an indication of whether a sizing discussion is needed at all (e.g., if there are no stories ready to be sized).

The discovery board can also serve as a to-do list so people who are focusing on the discovery process can determine which backlog items they need to get ready next. It also provides a clue to other team members that they need to help out to make sure the team has enough backlog items ready for the next iteration planning.

It is often helpful to have a member of the team accept the responsibility for moving backlog items across the board and having the discussions with team members and stakeholders necessary to get the right backlog items (i.e., the ones that produce the most value when completed) ready for the next iteration.

Finally, it's very helpful to have the discovery board and the delivery board[76] next to each other so the team can do their daily coordination discussions (stand-ups) at the boards. This focuses their discussions on items in play on either the discovery board or the delivery board instead of having people say what they did, what they are doing, and what obstacles are in their way.

How is a business analyst involved?

As a business analyst, you typically facilitate the discussion with your team to determine the appropriate order based on implementation concerns, and identify aspects of the solution that

---

[76] https://www.kbp.media/delivery-board/

help you get closer to your desired outcome. You can and should make this decision, especially if you're fulfilling the product owner role.

How to build and deliver the solution

Based on how user stories are described, your team repeatedly makes decisions that determine the best way to implement those stories.

Helpful techniques

There are numerous techniques that your team can use to determine how to go about building the preferred solution. When exploring these decisions from a business analyst's perspective, I've focused on the techniques that are most useful for providing the information the team needs to make those decisions. The discussion in Chapter 9 about describing user stories explains the types of decisions you and your team make on a daily basis.

How is a business analyst involved?

As a business analyst you typically keep the desired outcome at the forefront of the team and build a shared understanding about the need and selected solution. You do that through properly describing user stories so that your team has the information they need to determine the best way to build and deliver the solution.

Whether there is enough to deliver

Your team should make this decision on a regular basis. It's how you determine whether you should deploy your most recent work.

You're trying to determine if the components you've built create a viable solution or a viable, workable change to what you already have that will contribute toward delivering the outcome you seek.

In some respects, you're applying acceptance criteria to a group of user stories that represent the solution as a whole.

Helpful techniques

The most helpful techniques for this decision help you determine whether you've delivered the user stories as you intended. Techniques that will provide some of that information include acceptance criteria[77] and a Definition of done.[78]

Acceptance criteria point to things that need to be in place in order for customers, users, or stakeholders to accept that the user story meets their needs. They are also a set of statements, each with a clear pass/fail result, that specify both functional and nonfunctional requirements and are applicable at a variety of levels (feature and user stories). You can think of acceptance criteria as telling you whether that part of the **product** is done.

If the relevant acceptance criteria are met, then you are in a good position to deliver. If not all the acceptance criteria are met, you probably have more work to do.

The Definition of done is an agreement on the set of conditions that need to be true in order to consider a backlog item done and at a point where it can deliver value to stakeholders. It often includes meeting acceptance criteria and the team's completion of other activities. Those activities usually include testing, documentation updates, and presence in certain environments. You can think of the Definition of done as telling you whether the key parts of your **process** are done.

The main purpose of the Definition of done is to establish agreement around the things the team wants to do and confirm for each user story before they consider the solution ready to release it to production.

---

[77] https://www.kbp.media/acceptance-criteria/
[78] https://www.kbp.media/definition-done/

When you are comfortable that each of the individual user stories you've delivered so far meets acceptance criteria and Definition of done, you then need to look at the collection of functionality that's been created and determine if the solution as a whole provides a workable, usable solution. In effect, will deploying what you have provide additional benefits to your customers and users?

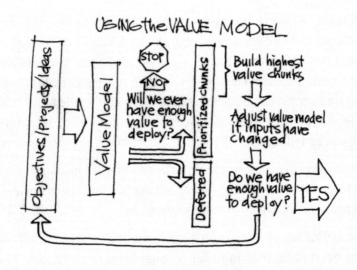

Figure 18. Using your Definition of done and acceptance criteria to decide when to deliver. Adopted from Stand Back and Deliver.

You may find in some cases that you don't have everything you need to in order to deploy a workable solution to your users so you need to build additional functionality.

In that case you can either hold off deploying, or you can employ a feature flag[79] approach which lets you deploy all the code that you've developed but turn off functionality that you don't want your users using just quite yet.

---

[79] https://martinfowler.com/articles/feature-toggles.html

How is a business analyst involved?

As a business analyst, you may be in a position to make this decision, especially if you are also playing product owner role. Even if you don't have direct responsibility for making the decision, you will most likely play a key role in confirming that what was built is viable.

Who decides

Throughout this discussion I noted the role typically responsible for making a given decision. It's important to realize that these are not hard and fast rules. Each situation will be different based on the makeup of your team, your organizational structure, and—let's face it— politics in your organization.

While I encourage you to use the suggestions in this chapter as guidelines, you're best off if you have a discussion with your team and the broader product organization to clarify decision responsibilities for your overall portfolio and each individual initiative.

The person responsible for product ownership should make sure decisions get made. That implies that if you are the one responsible for product ownership, you are not going to make all the decisions yourself.

The person who makes a specific decision should be as informed as possible and should be in a position to make the decisions stick. That's usually the person closest to the work. So if you follow this line of thinking, spread decision making out into the organization.

That said, decision making is most effective when a single person makes a decision, rather than a committee.

So how do you address this seeming paradox? The key is to identify the one person who makes each specific kind of decision and realize that different people will make different decisions.

You will own some of those decisions, members of your organization's leadership and members of your team will own others. It's helpful to discuss decision-making responsibility when your team starts work on a product and revisit those responsibilities when conditions or team members change.

So even though you don't own all the decisions, you should own making sure your team has determined who owns each decision.

One good way to determine who should decide is to use a framework such as DACI[80] to identify everyone's role in making a particular type of decision. DACI stands for the four roles people can play in relation to decisions:

Driver. This is the person responsible for making sure a decision gets made. In most cases this is one of the product people working on the product, so you may find yourself being the driver more often than not. There will only be one driver per type of decision and they will most often have to shepherd everyone else involved in the decision, make sure the key information is available, and make sure the decision is made in a timely fashion.

Approver. This is the one person who actually makes the decision. (I think the word "approver" is used so that DACI is pronounceable.) You'll only have one person per decision, and you'll want to make sure they have the authority and information necessary to make an informed decision.

Contributors. These are the people that have information or expertise relevant to the decision, although they don't necessarily get a vote in the final outcome. You can think of these folks (there can be more than one) as having a voice, but no vote.

---

[80] https://www.atlassian.com/team-playbook/plays/daci

Informed. These are the people who are directly affected by the decision and should be informed of the final decision.

Identify who is in each role for a given type of decision before you're faced with a decision, so you can determine the roles when everyone is calm and still likes each other. This also keeps decisions about the approver from being influenced by the desired outcome of a particular decision.

When to decide

Most people dislike uncertainty. They would rather take the risk of making a wrong decision now than live with the uncertainty for as long as necessary to improve their chances of making the right decision later. Instead of making a decision right away with limited information, determine when that decision needs to be made, in terms of either time or the conditions that need to be met. In the intervening time, collect and investigate information that improves your chances of making the right decision.

How do you determine the appropriate time to decide?

Most decisions involve selecting from a set of options, each of which is available to you for only a certain amount of time. You have until right before the first option disappears to make your decision, gathering information in the meantime. Even then, you may not need to make a final decision; you really only have to decide if you want to go with the expiring option or would rather use a different option.

How to decide

Decision making can be a vague concept, so here's some structure to help explain how to approach the act of making a decision:

- Select a decision mechanism.
- Determine what information you need.
- Build support with peers/stakeholders.
- Communicate the decision.
- Enact the decision.

Select a decision mechanism

Knowing who is going to make a decision impacts the mechanism used to make the decision. Constraints such as how much time you want to spend and how much collaboration you feel is necessary can also impact your approach.

You can use the combination of those two characteristics to guide your selection of approach.

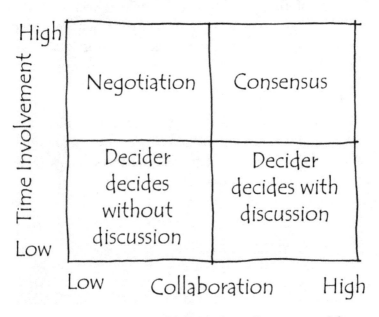

Figure 19. The amount of time you're willing to spend for a decision and the need for collaboration may influence how a decision is made.

Negotiation

Low collaboration, High time involvement

You'll often see a negotiation approach to decision making when there are groups of people that hold opposing viewpoints. These groups also tend to see the situation as a zero-sum game where if one group wins, the other will lose. When you follow a negotiation approach to decision making, each party gives up something in an attempt to find a solution that everyone can live with but that no one finds ideal. The more that politics are prevalent in your organization, the more likely you'll see this approach.

Consensus

High collaboration, high time involvement

This is the type of decision making where everyone has to agree and buy into the decision. Getting to that point can often take quite a while depending on the stakes involved. Some organizations pride themselves on being collaborative decision makers, but this can often lead to a dysfunction that results in no decisions being made.

Decider decides without discussion

Low collaboration, low time involvement

This is a dictatorship. It also can quickly lead to a very dysfunctional situation. If you use this approach too many times you may make some good decisions initially without taking advice from others. But eventually the lack of input can lead to uninformed, and potentially disastrous, decisions. There are some situations where this approach makes sense, especially if the decider is the only expert in the particular subject.

Decider decides with discussion

High collaboration, low time involvement

In this approach, the decider ultimately makes decisions themselves, but they gather information pertinent to the decision before deciding which way to go.

If you're going to use this approach, it's a good idea to have a discussion using the DACI framework described above to understand who needs to be involved.

This approach works when the decider talks with key stakeholders to get their perspectives and understand the possible options, and then makes the decision based on a synthesis of the information gathered.

Determine what information you need

To make an informed decision, determine what information you need. That will vary based on the decision you're making; mental models[81] can help you structure the information needed for any given decision.

For example, in *Stand Back and Deliver,* Pollyanna, Niel, Todd, and I discussed the business value model,[82] which we've found very helpful for identifying and organizing the information necessary to make many of the significant product-related decisions I mentioned above.

When you pull information together to help you make a decision, do so in a way that helps you to counteract cognitive biases—patterns of deviation in judgment that occur in particular situations.

Build support with peers/stakeholders

Your decision-making method impacts how much time you need to spend building support with your peers and other stakeholders once you make the decision.

---

[81] https://www.kbp.media/mental-models-help-make-decisions/
[82] https://www.kbp.media/business-value-models/

If you decided by consensus, you already have the support of everyone involved in making the decision. Deciding with the input of others will help you build support, especially if you listened to and considered input from the key people whose support you need.

If you are the sole decision maker, you have a bit more work on your hands. If you make decisions in a dictatorial manner, you may have a harder time building support and may never fully win the support of everyone involved.

Communicate the decision

Once you make a decision, you should make sure that those you expect to be involved in enacting the decision, and those impacted by it, know about it. The way you communicate the decision may be a key aspect of how you build support, especially for those stakeholders who wouldn't normally expect to be involved in making the decision.

Enact the decision

When making a decision, it's best to think about how it will be enacted at the same time. The execution of a decision can play a huge part in whether it produces the results envisioned by the person or people making the decision.

Evaluating your decision

Once you've made and enacted a decision you should reflect on it and see how you did. Determine if the decision was right by comparing the actual outcomes with the objective you were targeting.

Evaluate the process you used to make sure that you had the information that you needed, and that you made the decision at the right time: not too early, so you didn't lose out on key information, and not too late, such that desirable options expired.

On a recent project, the team decided to switch up our approach to building new features that were full stack (including both a user interface and back-end elements). Before, we had always tried to do stories that included the full stack but had run into several occasions where those stories took a full two or three weeks to complete.

This time, we agreed that someone would lay out all the front-end elements as a spike without test driving them, then the team would start implementing the various user stories that delivered the actual functionality. We had not used this approach in the past because you couldn't really test the initial work.

To evaluate our decision, we talked about what we experienced at the next retrospective. We discussed as a team how the experience went and whether we would repeat that approach again in a similar situation.

Having that follow-up discussion allowed us to assess the effectiveness of the decision and gauge whether we would make a similar decision in the future.

CHAPTER 11 – HOW TO USE SHORT FEEDBACK CYCLES TO LEARN

In Chapter 2, I quoted the opening of the Manifesto for Agile Software Development: "We are uncovering better ways of developing software by doing it and helping others do it." While some think that is merely intended as a preamble, I agree with Chris Matts that the first line of the Agile Manifesto **is the manifesto**. The rest is just a status report.

A lot of the practices, techniques, and ideas that surround agile are about learning. Learning from experience, not learning through navel-gazing and hand-waving (although the latter approach has worked for some framework marketers as of late).

While you learn about a lot of things when you work in an agile fashion, you're typically learning in two main areas—what you're building (your product) and how your team goes about building it (your team's methodology). Because you prize learning so much, you want a way to do it as much as possible so you look for ways to experience short feedback cycles.

This chapter reviews some of the ways you can use short feedback cycles to learn about your product and methodology, as well as some ways to go about learning new techniques.

Product feedback

Teams use iterative approaches, either timeboxed sprints or single-piece flow, to get frequent and rapid feedback. The premise is simple: the most useful feedback you can get happens when people actually use your product. You can ask them about it, but more importantly you can see how they use it and see the results of using it via changes in their behavior.

So it stands to reason that the best way to learn from feedback is to deliver your product as early as you can and then observe the impact on your chosen outcome based metric.

If your metric hits your defined target, you can stop work on that particular outcome and focus on a different one.

If your metric starts making progress toward your target but doesn't quite get there, you can decide what additional changes you need to make.

If your metric starts heading toward your constraint—the point that you didn't want to get to, you have to decide if you should back out the change you made and try something different.

Getting feedback before you build

There is certainly some truth to the idea that the only way to get truly useful feedback is to build something and show it to your users—or better yet, let them use it. But there is some value to showing your users prototypes: you can get feedback that prevents you from building something that is clearly not going to fit their way of working.

I experienced that firsthand on a recent project where we were rebuilding a tool used to manage the price of production inputs. One of the processes this product supported required users to enter several local price points. The team originally decided to provide a list of price points for users to maintain; when they needed to add or edit prices, they would click on the appropriate line item to open a modal window and make the changes.

The team created a prototype to demonstrate that approach and showed it to our users. They did not like it.

At all.

They told us in no uncertain terms that it would be a pain to have a separate window open up every time you had to add a line item or make an edit because you'd have to do several at the same time.

This was a very good thing. Although we had spent some time putting the prototype together, we saved the team a considerable amount of work by not having them build the modal approach. Granted, we could have probably saved even more time by sketching the idea on a whiteboard and discussing it with our users. All the same, it was still a win.

The moral of the story is that there is some value in doing a little bit of design and describing user stories before you start building them, as long as you discuss your ideas with your stakeholders. If you present the information in a way that's meaningful to your customers, users, and stakeholders you may be able to avoid building unnecessary functionality.

Getting feedback before you deliver

I've described the ideal way to get product feedback. Sometimes you want feedback before you deliver, or to help you to decide when to deliver. And sometimes you aren't in a position to easily measure impact from delivering a product to production.

The Scrum framework includes the sprint review event to make sure you get feedback on a regular basis.

Sprint reviews exist primarily to get feedback from your stakeholders when you can't get feedback from them during a sprint, and to help you decide if you have enough to deliver.

Note I didn't say that they are to get feedback from the product owner. A product owner should provide feedback along the way so your team has a shorter feedback cycle and has an opportunity to act on the feedback you provide within that sprint. If the product owner is surprised during a sprint review by something the team discusses, something is wrong.

With that thought in mind, here are some frequently asked questions about sprint reviews, answered from a product ownership perspective.

Should we always do sprint reviews?

Should you always look for feedback?

Okay, a little snarky I'll admit.

If the product owner has already provided feedback during the sprint, and if you were able to get feedback from the key stakeholders interested in what the team was working on, you may not need a sprint review. You already have the feedback, so may just be doing the sprint review because that's what teams do at the end of sprints. Unless, of course, you are using a flow approach, in which case you better be getting feedback after every item is done.

My guideline: Do you need more feedback? Do a sprint review.

If you miss an important outcome metric, it may be time for re-planning. If you keep hitting targets, all is good and you may not need feedback.

If nothing we have is visible to stakeholders (customers), do we still do a demo?

Some teams (teams working in a mainframe environment or teams with a large, complex code base come to mind) may find themselves working on stuff that provides value to stakeholders or customers, but is not very demonstrable. If this describes your team, look for a good way to get feedback on the work you did. Mainframe teams I worked with have used before and after screenshots. Admittedly not very exciting, but it was enough to get the point across and to generate conversation and encourage feedback.

My guideline: Do you need more feedback? Do a sprint review. Figure out how to show something meaningful to get that feedback.

Who should attend sprint reviews?

It's good for the entire team to attend. This is not some "agile mandate"—there is no such thing—but it's helpful for the entire team to hear the feedback you're getting from stakeholders so they better understand what stakeholders are looking for. Also, different people may pick up on different things.

It's also helpful to consider which stakeholders have an interest in the stories the team is working on during the sprint. This is a good discussion to have during sprint planning. That way, you can specifically invite the people with a vested interest in those backlog items, instead of creating a blanket invitation to hundreds of people who may, possibly, be interested in what you are doing, sometime. You'll have more engaged attendees at your sprint review this way. Plus, this is more respectful of everyone's time and calendars.

Remember, whomever you invite, don't make it hard for them to give feedback.

My guideline: Include anyone that you need feedback from or who would benefit from hearing their feedback.

Who should do the sprint review?

It depends what you are trying to accomplish (beyond receiving feedback) and the makeup of your team.

I've seen the developers demo their own stories. This is good if you'd like to get some recognition for the developers and they won't go off the rails and give a 30-minute discourse on the nasty details of how they completed the story.

I've seen analysts or testers facilitate the sprint review. This is usually the case when they have a strong relationship with the stakeholders and the team feels that they can best convey what the team accomplished.

I've seen product owners facilitate the sprint review, for the same reason analysts or testers do it. Just make sure the product owner isn't doing the demo because they don't trust the team to do it properly. This is a sign of a dysfunctional relationship with your team.

I've seen members of the business unit who are working closely with the team facilitate the sprint review. This is often a form of subtle organizational change management. If other members of a team see someone from their team using the new solution, they conclude that it must not be that scary after all and is something they could use.

Perhaps the stakeholders should just play around with the software during the sprint review. In fact, that may be the most effective way of getting meaningful feedback, and it's certainly something to consider if your solution is in a state that stakeholders could start using. Observing users while they try to perform some task is one of the best ways of getting feedback.

If stakeholders play with software, the task of the team is to observe and identify gaps in understanding and come up with ideas on how to improve the software.

My guideline: The person who is best positioned to ensure you receive the most useful feedback is the one who should do the sprint review.

Some product feedback considerations

The need for feedback is rarely questioned these days, and has been suggested as far back as Winston Royce's paper on

Managing the Development of Large Software Systems[83] (hint, look at Figure 3 on the third page).

You want to get feedback early and often so you can quickly see if you are heading down a path that will satisfy your stakeholder's needs. Compare this to using a printed set of directions from Google Maps versus navigating using a GPS that includes information on road construction and current traffic.

A list of directions is certainly helpful for getting from where you are to your desired destination, and they can be even more helpful when you are not familiar with the destination or the space in between. Directions printed from Google Maps, MapQuest, or similar applications take advantage of the best information available at the time you print them, but they do not take advantage of current information while you drive. You may follow the directions exactly and still find yourself staring at a road that was closed because a bridge got knocked out by a semi that was too tall. Similarly, projects that start with the assumption that you can do all of your planning at the beginning and rely on those directions throughout provide a good picture based on what you knew when you created the plan, but later events reduce the usefulness of that plan.

Driving with a GPS provides you with the most current information because the GPS continuously collects information (feedback) about current road construction and traffic levels between you and your destination. It also responds (some more insistently than others) when you happen to take a wrong turn and gets you back on track. You may not end up taking your originally planned path to get to your destination, but you will get there. Iterative approaches regularly provide new information and allow you to revise your approach. With frequent feedback and up-to-date information, you can decide whether changes in your approach are necessary to get to your ultimate destination.

---

[83] http://www.serena.com/docs/agile/papers/Managing-The-Development-of-Large-Software-Systems.pdf

There are some subtleties in getting that frequent feedback that are worth discussing.

Don't rely exclusively on the sprint review

Sprint reviews give you a chance to demonstrate functionality you've created, but that experience rarely produces the richest feedback. What does? Letting people use the product themselves. Your demonstration will inevitably provide a sanitized view of the product's function. You are probably avoiding the little imperfections when you demo it in a sprint review. This may leave a good impression but it doesn't contribute to real learning.

You're much more likely to get a better understanding of whether your product will deliver the outcome you're hoping for by giving your users the chance to use it in a setting where they can try things out without major, business-impacting repercussions.

In addition, if you are replacing an existing product, you may find it helpful to run the current product and your new product in parallel for a while before switching over. That's the best way to confirm that your new product delivering the outcome you want.

Feedback from those who disagree with you is important

When I was in the final stages of writing *Beyond Requirements: Analysis with an Agile Mindset*, I sent a draft of the book to several experts for review. Five people graciously read through the manuscript and provided very helpful feedback. Getting their feedback before the book was finalized helped me get a reading on whether the book was on target.

Some of most helpful feedback was from someone I'll call Bob the Book Reviewer. It was immediately apparent that my outlook on the world of IT projects and Bob's were quite different.

While there were many aspects of the book he liked, there were a few things that he was adamantly opposed to. I was all set to disregard most of his comments, but before I did, I ran them by one of my mentors. I was hoping that my mentor would tell me that I was right to ignore the feedback. Instead, the mentor said that in several cases Bob had a good point.

I'm not proud that I was about to discount feedback that didn't agree with my worldview, but I am glad that I got a second opinion before I did so.

Thoughtfully considering Bob's feedback helped me to explain some of the concepts covered in the book in a way that (hopefully) makes sense to those who don't necessarily share my assumptions. I believe the book is stronger and a more useful resource as a result.

You need to pay attention to feedback from those who disagree with you or that do not completely support your product. Their feedback often identifies weaknesses in your work that people who share your beliefs may not point out, or may not see themselves. That's not to say that you are going to follow their advice. You can't do that with anyone. But you should at least consider their feedback and think about where it's coming from. Understanding the inspiration for their comments may help you find weaknesses in your efforts.

Don't overlook different sources of feedback

You may be tempted to ignore some stakeholders because they disagree with you. Others you just may not think of as having actionable feedback. Don't discount these stakeholders; they may have unique relationships with your users or customers that can generate some very helpful information.

I had the opportunity to work with the tech support team in a software product company. Tech Support wanted to understand agile software development better so they could interact more effectively with Engineering and Product Management. During the discussions I realized they had a lot of great information about how users actually used their product and the problems users often ran into. Engineering invited Tech Support to their demos to get feedback on new functionality but did not engage with Tech Support about what features to deliver in the first place. To be fair, Tech Support was not providing that type of information to Product Management or Engineering either. No one involved realized that information from Tech Support could be useful for making roadmap and priority decisions.

Look for feedback from different parts of your organization, keeping in mind the relationship each part has with your customers and users. It's also important to remember those relationships as you expand the sources of your feedback to properly consider all of that information as a whole, including information you get from sources other than people.

Feedback does not always have to come from people

I helped another organization with their inception planning efforts to determine their main focus for the next three months. We used a variation of impact mapping to determine the most valuable features to work on based on their key objectives.

One feature that rose to the top of the list did not appear on any of the existing product management roadmaps. The team realized that they needed to collect information about how (or whether) their customers were using certain functionality. This is a kind of feedback, and it's an important supplement to the feedback the team gets from their customers. It gave them a way to validate assumptions and confirm or question what their customers were telling them.

Even when you have a good relationship with your customers, you should always be a little skeptical about what they tell you. Brandon Carlson discussed this idea in his conference session Stop Listening to Your Customers.[84] Don't take this to mean that you shouldn't listen to your customers at all. It's best to practice the moderation: balance talking with your customers and analyzing hard data on usage.

As with the organization that wanted to collect more usage information, you may find that some extra work is required to record that information. That work may not initially be very high on the priority list of features, but it's still very important to do for the long-term health and success of the product. Think of it as an investment to aid future planning.

Set the expectations of those giving you feedback

Finally, set the proper expectations with those providing the feedback. There's a good chance that you will get a lot of feedback, some of which contradicts each other. That is to be expected and is fine. However, in order to make sure that you can continue to get feedback from those people, it's important to let them know that you appreciate their feedback and will consider it seriously, but you may not use all (or any) of it. Without setting those expectations, you run the risk of not being able to get feedback from those individuals in the future.

An example of product feedback

One of my favorite aspects of adopting an agile mindset is the tendency to think about whether what I am doing actually adds value to the organization. With this, though, comes the knotty problem that value can often be hard to clearly define. Because I generally find myself working on internal IT projects, I've resorted to measuring value based on the project objectives.

---

[84] http://www.infoq.com/news/2012/08/agile2012-stop-listening-cust

However, as I develop a better understanding of the agile mindset, an interesting thing happens—I do not always end up using value per se as the deciding factor of whether or not to do something. Sometimes I do things because it will help the team learn.

We'd like to think that we can clearly foresee everything when working on projects, especially when it comes to whether or not we fully understand the need we're trying to satisfy and the solutions that will satisfy that need. Unfortunately, we don't always bother to figure out the real need (or the real problem) and we're not always sure about the right solution. This is where learning comes in handy.

When working on a new initiative, it's common to think we've uncovered the problem we're trying to solve, but we're not always sure what the right solution is. When we find ourselves in this situation, the best thing to do is note what assumptions we're making—not simply because it's a good thing to do, but so we can identify the things needed to verify that we actually are delivering the right solution. (This scenario assumes we haven't been handed a solution by our stakeholders, in which case we should be asking whether that is really the right solution or if it's just a solution in search of a problem.)

It's long been held that it's good practice to identify the assumptions a team makes when working on a project, but the "good practice" seems to stop there. No real discussion occurs about what to do with the knowledge of those assumptions.

You need to identify the key assumptions that, if proven false, will shoot huge holes in the solution. These are not the "we assume that all the key players will be available" type of assumptions. More often, they tend to be of the "if we build it, they will come" nature.

These are also particularly insidious assumptions in cases where people have the choice of whether or not to use the solution, and this happens in internal IT situations more frequently than you care to believe. You could try to validate those assumptions by asking the stakeholders whether they will use the solution, but—warning!—you may not like the answer. And if you do, you may not like their corresponding action (or lack thereof). In many cases, the people you ask are going to lie to you. They're not doing it to be malicious; usually they think they are telling you what you want to hear. Unfortunately, their actions rarely match up.

When I find myself in these situations, I like to build something that will allow me to find out how a solution could affect people's behavior. This can be a very simple implementation of functionality, or it can be something as simple as a message in an email. Because I'm building this more for learning than with a lot of certainty that it's the solution, I don't make it too extravagant. I do the minimum necessary to find out how people will respond.

For example, the first couple of years we used the Agile Alliance Conference Submission System we had a problem with people misunderstanding the purpose of email notifications. In our effort to make the submission process interactive, we provided the capability for submitters and reviewers to carry on conversations via the submission system. A submitter would submit a session proposal, a reviewer would provide feedback and occasionally ask questions, and then the submitter could respond to the reviewer. The intent was for this conversation to occur all through the submission system interface. We provided the ability for everyone involved in these conversations to get a notice when their session proposal had received a review or their review had received comment. At first these emails just contained a link back to the submission system where the submitter or reviewer could reply. However, we received a request to include the content of the review or comment in the email notification so people could read it without having to go to the submission system. We assumed that the link saying "Please reply to this comment in the submission system" would be enough to drive that behavior. It wasn't.

As soon as emails started going out with the review text included, the general submission system email account started getting inundated with people replying to the emails instead of using the submission system. Our assumption that people would follow clear though somewhat subtle instructions turned out to be false. Once we realized what was going on, we made a further assumption that clearer, more obvious instructions would drive the right behavior. One alternative was a larger effort to setup the submission system to receive the replies and add them to the conversation in the submission system. This would have been a lot of work, so we tested the simpler method first: We added a message at the beginning of every notification email in big, bold letters.

Messages sent to this email address (submissions@agilealliance.org) do not go to Track Chairs or Reviewers. Please provide any replies to this review via the submission system.

We found this message reduced the number of simple email replies we got, but did not entirely stop them. We then decided that some gentle chastisement might work, so I responded to each email reply with a reminder that they needed to reply in the submission system. This was a little extra work on my behalf, but I found that once people got one "friendly reminder" they tended to use the system as intended.

In this case, we changed the notification message explicitly to test behavior change. The actual coding effort was extremely small, but it was enough to find out what would happen, and it gave us sufficient information to decide what we needed to do going forward.

You always build to provide value, but sometimes while you're heading in that direction you need to build some things to be sure you understand what value you are providing and whether the solution you're delivering provides it. The willingness to learn gives you a lot of freedom to experiment, validate your assumptions, confirm that the solution you are providing really is the right one. Those short detours are much better in the long run than blindly heading down the wrong path.

Trust me, I've done both in my day.

Methodology feedback

Ideally, your team is mature enough that when someone notices that you're not working as well together as you could, you talk it over and identify what the issue may be. Then, you decide what you want to try to change, try it, and see what happens.

In reality, the vast majority of teams need to set aside time on a regular basis to force that kind of discussion. That's where retrospectives come into play. Regular retrospectives give your team a chance to establish a nice reflect and adapt cadence.

Unfortunately, retrospectives can easily become one of those things teams do because the framework and the coach said they should. They don't take them seriously, so they don't get the results out of the activity that they should. Worse yet, the team checks out because they don't get any value out of retrospectives and the scrum master resorts to gimmicks and games to keep the team interested. Retrospectives become agile theater.

That's where *action focused retrospectives* come in.

Action focused retrospectives are a way for your team to reflect on your past cycle of work, discuss what you've learned, identify specific action items to pursue, and follow through on those action items.

Action focused retrospectives typically follow this structure (from *Agile Retrospectives* by Esther Derby and Diana Larsen):

- Set the stage
- Gather data

- Generate insights
- Decide what to do
- Wrap up

When to use action focused retrospectives

It's a healthy practice for your team to pause periodically, reflect on your work, and determine opportunities for improvement or experiments you want to try.

If your team works in an iterative fashion (such as sprints using the Scrum framework) the usual timing is at the end of each cycle (sprint).

If your team works in a flow fashion (for example, Kanban) it's helpful to have a recurring checkpoint to reflect and adapt—this may be every week or two, depending on how fast-paced your team's environment is.

Why use action focused retrospectives

Retrospectives are an important activity for your team to deliberately practice continuous improvement. Without a clearly defined reflection point, your team may fall into a pattern where they continue to work in the same fashion, continue to run into the same obstacles, and never learn from the experiences to improve their work moving forward.

Failure to use retrospectives prevents your team from having explicit approaches to clearing obstacles, identifying opportunities for improvement, and identifying experiments to try out new approaches.

Use an action focused approach to retrospectives to ensure that your retrospective discussions generate action and follow up rather than just being a forum for your team to air their gripes.

How to do action focused retrospectives

Set the stage. Gather the team together and remind everyone that the purpose of the retrospective is to reflect on the past week(s), discuss what happened and what you can learn from that, and determine specific action(s) for moving forward.

It's also good to remind everyone of the Retrospective Prime Directive from Norm Kerth (Project Retrospectives: A Handbook for Team Review[85]):

> Regardless of what we discover, we understand and truly believe that everyone did the best job they could, given what they knew at the time, their skills and abilities, the resources available, and the situation at hand.

Another good thing to do at this point is to review any action items that were established at the previous retrospectives and discuss the results. This is a good way to ensure follow up on action items and provides a nice transition to the next step.

Gather data. Ask team members to individually write thoughts on sticky notes about the past sprint or week(s) based on a set of topics. One thought per sticky note, as many sticky notes as they want.

There are a variety of sets of topics that teams can use, including:

- Good, Bad, Meh
- Start, Stop, Continue
- What went well, what did we learn, what should we do differently, what still puzzles us

There's no magic in which set of topics you use. Find one that works for your team and run with it. You may find that you need to change up the topics if the team gets tired of them.

---

[85] https://amzn.to/2NFx4Mr

Once everyone identifies their items, ask them to put their sticky notes up on the whiteboard under the appropriate topic. Ask everyone on the team to do this at the same time so the source of specific notes is not immediately obvious. This should encourage your team members to be more forthcoming with their thoughts.

The resulting whiteboard will look something like this:

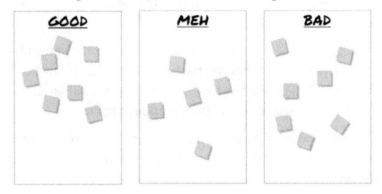

Figure 20. An action focused retrospective whiteboard.

Generate Insights. Start with *affinity grouping*. Once everyone has put their thoughts up on the board, ask your team to group the ideas in each topic into similar categories. Try to avoid leaving any "orphan" sticky notes standing alone. Don't move any notes between topics.

This gives your team the chance to see all the ideas and how their ideas relate to the thoughts of others on the team.

After affinity grouping, the board may look like this.

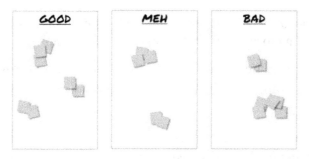

Figure 21. An action focused retrospective after affinity grouping.

Once you all the sticky notes are in affinity groups, ask your team to **suggest a title for each group**. You can either have someone from the team do this as the team does the affinity grouping, or you (as the facilitator) can quickly go group to group and ask what title you should write. If you take this approach, I've found it helpful to read the sticky notes in the group and then ask the team for title suggestions. You may find that you have to suggest titles.

Don't spend too long identifying titles for each group, but make sure the team is aware of the general theme of each group and that you come up with a title that appropriately describes that theme.

Once you have titles, the board will look something like this:

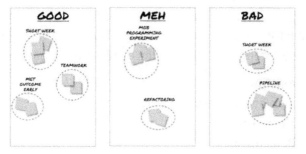

Figure 22. With the retrospective items grouped, have the team suggest a title for each group that reflects its theme.

Next, ask your team to indicate which topics they would like to discuss in more detail by **dot voting** on the groups.

A good heuristic for determining the number of votes each person gets is to count the number of groups, divide by three and round up.

In this case there are seven groups, so dividing by three and rounding up results in three votes per person. There are seven team members, so there will be a total of 21 votes.

Each person can choose where to put their votes. They can put all of their votes on one group or spread them out to multiple groups.

The board may look like this as a result.

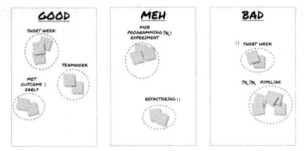

Figure 23. An action focused retrospective board after dot voting. Because Pipeline received the most votes, it will be discussed first.

The team then uses these votes to determine the order in which you discuss items. In this case, the order of topics is:

1. Pipeline
2. Mob programming experiment
3. Short week
4. Refactoring
5. Met outcome early

For each topic, your team discusses the story behind the group of sticky notes and why the group of notes is sitting in the particular topic.

These discussions give your team a chance to clarify the concerns the rest of the team has or the assumptions the rest of the team is making. They also tend to blur the lines between gathering insights and deciding what to do, as the discussions will often identify potential action items.

If you find that your team tends to linger on an issue, preventing you from covering all the topics you want to discuss in the retrospective, you may want to timebox the discussion. When you reach a set limit for an issue you can choose to continue the discussion, identify action items for that issue, or just stop discussion of that issue.

For some discussions, you'll want to clearly identify a specific action item, especially those that appear in the Bad column. In the example shown in Figure 23, the team was having a bit of difficulty with their development pipeline, so the outcome of the discussion on that topic should identify some action steps they can take to resolve the pipeline issues.

For other discussions, you may discuss the results of an experiment that your team tried for the time period that the retrospective covered (the team in this running example tried mob programming in the previous sprint). In that case, your team may decide whether to continue the experiment, abandon the practice, or adopt the practice on an ongoing basis.

Finally, the intent of some discussions is just to comment on some good things that happened and give kudos to the team. Your team may also want to discuss what made that something successful and identify what actions you can repeat in other situations.

Decide what to do. Identify specific actions that your team can take to benefit from or address the situation you are discussing. While you need to spend a little time making sure the team has a shared understanding about the scenario and its consequences, drive toward identifying action items rather than just falling into an ongoing complaint session. As the team identifies action items, make note of them (the best way to do that is to write them on the board near the sticky notes describing the particular situation).

As you near the end of your scheduled time for the retrospective, or if you have made it through all the identified discussion topics, explicitly ask the team to select which action item they plan to tackle in the next sprint or week(s).

It's best to focus on a very small number of action items—preferably one—to increase the chances that your team will finish that item. The more items your team tries to tackle, the bigger the chance the team does not accomplish any of the action items.

Once you've selected the action item, identify who will own making sure the action item is completed, when it should be completed (usually by the next retrospective), and the criteria for knowing it is successfully completed.

If you choose to tackle multiple action items, identify the same information for each action item.

Wrap up. Finally, confirm that your team has a shared understanding about the action items coming out of the meeting.

Ask if anyone has any comments about the process you used for the retrospective (a retrospective on the retrospective as it were).

You may also want to see if there were any topics that weren't discussed that someone has a burning desire to bring up. Depending on the dynamics of the group you may need to be careful with this, but it can often help people to know there is always an opportunity to bring something up that they just thought of or didn't include in the initial data gathering.

Caveats and considerations

You may decide to have each person read off their sticky notes as they put them up so that everyone hears every point. If some team members are reluctant to bring things up if they are directly associated with the idea, then it's best to have everyone put their sticky notes up at the same time. If that concern is a factor, you have a significant team dynamics issue that you need to work through.

The definite advantage to having everyone put their sticky notes up at the same time is that it is faster than having each person read each sticky note. If you have everyone put their notes up at the same time, you'll want to provide an opportunity for the team to read through all the notes. The affinity grouping exercise provides that opportunity.

There are a variety of different approaches to setting the stage, gathering data, and generating insights provided in the book *Agile Retrospectives: Making Good Teams Great* by Esther Derby and Diana Larsen. You may want to check those approaches out if your team is facing a challenging situation or you've been using the approach described above for a long time and your retrospectives are becoming monotonous.

You may want to focus discussions on specific categories of sticky note topics. For example, in the case described in this chapter, you may ask the team to focus on the "Meh" and the "Bad" topics. This is a judgment call. There is some value in discussing the good things that happened, especially if there is the need to increase the frequency or intensity of a particular activity.

It may help to have someone from outside your team facilitate the retrospective (such as a coach or an experienced facilitator from a different team). This allows everyone on the team to focus on the content of the retrospective and allows for an unbiased facilitator. This is not a requirement, but it may be handy on occasion, to provide a different perspective.

How to learn things when you need to

With the vast number of techniques out there, it's possible to become a professional student and spend all your time learning about new techniques, becoming an expert in every one. That's not necessarily what I'm suggesting here. Rather, I think it's important to be aware of the variety of techniques available, when to use them, and how to quickly get up to speed on them when you need to. Here's how I do that.

Keep an eye out for new techniques

There are two categories of new techniques for business analysts:

1) Techniques that are new to you but are practiced by other members of your team.

2) New analysis techniques that make you more effective.

It's easy to decide when to do the first type of technique—usually someone on your team has hit a bottleneck and needs some help to keep things moving. If you have some time available, or if the work you're currently doing is not as time-critical, you can be a good team member and help. Hopefully, learning that new technique will also help you be better at business analysis. That was the situation I was in when working on a data warehouse project as a project manager/business analyst and found myself reverse engineering COBOL code to elicit business rules and modeling data and developing SQL stored procedures. I primarily did those activities because they needed to get done, but they also added skills to my toolkit that I use to this day.

Deciding when to pick up new analysis techniques can be trickier. You need to balance seeking continuous improvement with not falling victim to the shiny object syndrome—where you think every new technique you hear about will solve all your problems. I know this happens because I've fallen into that trap more often than I care to admit. What I have found works best is to find some people I trust and respect and listen to what they are talking about. This works best when you follow people that you know are practitioners, because when they share their stories you know they are sharing things they have done. I compiled a list of Product Ownership blogs and newsletters[86]on my blog that I follow to find out about new techniques. That list is primarily product management and UX focused, because those types of techniques are very helpful for business analysts.

When you come across a new technique, make sure you understand what outcome the technique produces, and when it is most applicable. If you explicitly look for this information, you may avoid falling victim to the shiny object syndrome.

The other thing I suggest is keeping a perspective of Just-In-Time instead of Just-In-Case learning. Just-In-Time learning means you find out what the technique is, know when it's appropriate to use, and know where to find more information. Organizations like the IIBA (in the BABOK Techniques section) and the Agile Alliance (in the Agile Glossary[87]) provide descriptions of techniques at a level appropriate to understand what the techniques are and when they are useful.

Just-In-Case learning means you go on a binge of downloading resources, buying books, and attending classes about a technique even though you aren't sure when or if you will use it.

When you do this, one of two things happens: You learn all this great info about this new technique, then don't find an opportunity to use it and promptly forget everything, or you learn all you can about the new technique and then walk around with a proverbial hammer in your hand and everything looks like a

---

[86] http://www.kbp.media/po_blogs_newsletters/
[87] https://www.agilealliance.org/agile101/agile-glossary/

nail. You can end up applying the technique to solve every problem you come across even when it's not a good fit. Don't do that.

Search for resources about how to do it

Once you find an appropriate use for a technique, it's time to do a deep dive. If you're learning a technique to help other team members, ask those team members what resources they suggest.

You can also do a targeted internet search where you ask about the technique in a specific context, such as: "Story mapping for health insurance business intelligence." If you don't find any useful resources with those specific searches, you can always broaden your search. Pick the results that describe actual experiences, rather than the resources that only explain the theory of the technique.

Wikipedia is a good place to start with information about the technique, but use it primarily to find out who initially created it or has expanded the use of the technique, then look up resources from those creators. The Agile Alliance Agile Glossary is also a good place to find links to other resources, both on the Agile Alliance site and off, that provide more information about some techniques.

Targeted questions on LinkedIn groups can also be helpful. Just be prepared to separate the people who have used the technique from those who have just read about it. Pay attention to people whose answers are like "when we tried this out I found" or "I usually like to do this ..." over those who respond with prescriptions such as: "The daily standup must always be 15 minutes or less and managers must not speak." When you find people with actual experience using the technique, reach out to them and pick their brains. Your own experience is the best teacher; others' experience is almost as good.

Finally, a particularly good source of resources relevant to this book is the resource page I've set up on the KBP.media website.

Books by their very nature are somewhat locked in time when they are published, but it's easy to keep web pages more up-to-date. As a result, I've created a resources page on KBP.Media that contains references relevant for every chapter and will be updated on an ongoing basis as I come across new resources. You can find it on the How to be an agile business analyst resources page.[88]

Establish a safety net

This is most appropriate when you learn a technique new to you but familiar to others in the team. Find someone on the team who is an expert in that technique who can either pair with you when you are doing the technique or review things before you finish them. Since you are probably doing a task to help someone who is too busy, you'll have to find a way to get this support that makes the best use of the other person's time.

When I was doing the SQL development for the data warehouse project, my safety net was Mike, a skilled SQL developer in our area. He had limited availability for the project, so I did the development work and testing in a test environment, and then went over it with him. It was important for me to find out not only where I had written bad code, but also why it was bad code. Finding that out helped me understand general principles of writing SQL code that I still remember to this day. The same idea applies for any technique you learn.

One approach that allows team members to learn techniques with a safety net is called Staff Liquidity.[89] Each member of the team assesses their abilities for a variety of techniques. Then, when the team is deciding who is going to work on what, the people who are less familiar with an activity volunteer for those

---

[88] https://www.kbp.media/agile-business-analyst-resources/
[89] https://theitriskmanager.wordpress.com/2013/11/24/introducing-staff-liquidity-1-of-n/

items first. That leaves more experienced people free to coach and mentor. This ensures that knowledge of key activities spreads throughout the team, and that the more experienced members are available to jump in when an urgent issue comes up without unduly impacting the work of the overall team.

Just do it

You can read about a technique and talk to others about how they've done it, but you really learn by doing it. You'll learn it even better if you make recoverable mistakes when trying the technique out. If there is a new technique that you think may be helpful, make sure it's appropriate in your situation and then try it. Start with the expectation that you may make some mistakes and be prepared to learn from those mistakes and figure out how you may do it differently in the future.

Limit the amount of time you spend trying a technique the first time. You don't want to spend a lot of time doing something without any feedback. Try something in a limited fashion, then get feedback on how the technique went, consider that feedback, and think about how it will impact what you do the next time.

When I was doing the SQL development, I would write a procedure or two, then run those procedures in test and check them with Mike to make sure I was heading down the right path. If I made a mistake at this point it was recoverable, because I was in a test environment.

These days I get the opportunity to expand my website building skills when I make changes to the Agile Alliance website. I pick an isolated instance of the new technique I'm trying, do it, then have some other members of the team look at the page and get their feedback.

If you are taking a course on the technique, make sure the course includes an opportunity to try out the technique—if not in your own context, at least on an example that is somewhat related.

Teach it to someone else

If you've used the technique, found it worked for you, and you think you are going to continue to use it, the best way to increase your knowledge and understanding is to teach it to someone else. The Feynman technique[90]—developed by Richard Feynman, a Nobel Prize–winning physicist known for his ability to explain complicated topics—is a great formula for learning anything:

1. Choose a concept
2. Teach it to a toddler
3. Identify gaps and go back to the source material
4. Review and simplify

Use the Feynman technique to describe the technique you have learned and tried. This will help other people learn it as well, at the same time making sure you really understand it.[91]

---

[90] https://www.farnamstreetblog.com/2012/04/learn-anything-faster-with-the-feynman-technique/
[91] https://www.farnamstreetblog.com/2015/09/two-types-of-knowledge/

Chapter 12 – The Business Analysis Process through an Agile Lens

Laura Brandenburg describes business analysis in terms of an eight-step process[92] which she uses as the foundation for her BA Essentials Master Class. In this chapter I'll look at each step through an agile lens, along with the key responsibilities associated with each step.

Here are the eight steps:

Step 1 - Get oriented

Step 2 - Discover the primary business objective

Step 3 - Define scope

Step 4 - Formulate your business analysis plan

Step 5 - Define the detailed requirements

Step 6 - Support the technical implementation

Step 7 - Help the business implement the solution

Step 8 - Assess value created by the solution

Step 1 – Get oriented

Whenever you start work on a new internal product, try to solve a problem you haven't dealt with before, or work with new stakeholders, resist the temptation to dive right into the effort. Take some time to get familiar with the context and the people involved.

---

[92] https://www.bridging-the-gap.com/business-analysis-process/

A small amount of time identifying the things you don't know you don't know and then learning about some of those things can pay huge dividends in the course of your work.

Don't spend so long getting familiar with your environment that you lose momentum. Try to keep your acclimation time to one or two weeks tops. If it makes sense to start sprinkling in work on your internal product, by all means do so.

So what do you do during this orientation time? Chris Matts and I described our approach in the chapter we wrote for the book *Business Analysis & Leadership: Influencing Change*. Here it is in the guise of an answer to the question, "What is the first thing you do on a project?"

There is no first thing we do on a project. There are a number of things which we do in an opportunistic manner to gather as much information about the project and its context as we possibly can:

1. *Get to know the people involved.*
2. *Understand "WHY" we are doing the project.*
3. *Understand "WHAT" we are trying to achieve.*
4. *Get something done.*

These items fit nicely into the first four steps of the business analysis process, so I'll explore each idea in a little more detail in the appropriate place.

Key responsibilities

Each of the eight steps of the business analysis process includes key responsibilities that come along with that step. Here are the key responsibilities for the get oriented step, viewed from an agile perspective.

Clarifying your role as the business analyst so that you are sure to create deliverables that meet stakeholder needs.

You may work on a cross-functional team where everyone is expected to contribute in a variety of ways, but where each of you has a certain specialty. In this setting it's important to come to a general agreement about what each person on the team is responsible for, as well as an understanding of who has the skills to help out in other areas.

If there is more than one product person on a team, it's especially important for you to decide who will own which product responsibilities. Use the four product ownership models described in Chapter 5 as a starting point to help you decide how to split up those responsibilities.

One key thing to note: the artifacts you produce are a means to an end (building shared understanding), not the end itself. Identify responsibilities based on activities that you need to do and decisions that must be made in order to deliver the outcome that your team seeks to deliver. You'll find that you'll have more discussions around "What do we need to do?" or "What do we need to decide?" than "What documents do we need to create?"

Determining the primary stakeholders to engage in defining the project's business objectives and scope, as well as any subject matter experts to be consulted early in the project.

The focus of your initiative is to deliver some outcome that benefits your organization's customers. When you're working on an internal product, that benefit is often indirect in nature and can be influenced by the people who will use the product, and by other people inside your organization. In all of this, it's important to understand the difference between customers, users, and stakeholders and how to work with each.

Customers. The extent to which you get to know your organization's customers depends on how directly your product impacts them. If there is a direct impact—for instance, if you're working on your organization's website or a mobile app—you'll want a fairly good understanding of your customers, their needs, and their problems. Meaningful interviews are extremely helpful. If your work is on an existing product, you can also look into customer feedback and usage data that you already have about that product.

Users. As you start work on your initiative, you want a good understanding of the people who use (or will use) your product. You want to get familiar with them, their environment, and their approach to work so that you can ensure your product allows them to complete their activities effectively in pursuit of the desired outcome.

There are a variety of techniques you can use to build an understanding of your users. Two that I've found particularly helpful are user modeling to identify the different types of users that exist and personas to get a deeper understanding of those different types of users. As with most other techniques, the act of performing the technique adds as much value as, if not more than, the end result.

If your product already exists, you may be able to learn more about your users and how they actually use the product by observing them in their own environment or including them in some usability testing.

Stakeholders. Stakeholders may or may not be directly involved in your initiative, but they are usually in a position to help move it along or severely impede its progress. That's one of the reasons Chris and I called out getting to know the people involved in your project as one of the first things we always do:

Getting to know people involved in a project goes beyond simply creating a stakeholder map to show who can influence the outcome. It means meeting the people and getting to know what they are like, how they interact with others, and give them a chance to learn about us. In particular we stress the importance of collaboration and focus on achieving results. Our favourite tool for getting to know someone is the humble cup of coffee. Ideally we go out of the office and meet in a coffee bar, but if we can't do that we will try to find an atrium or cafe, and as a last resort a meeting room.

Don't take this to mean that stakeholder maps are not helpful. They are. The point is that they provide a good structure upon which you can build conversations in order to understand your stakeholders. Don't think that creating a map by itself is going to get you all the way there.

Another technique that will help you understand your stakeholders better, and know how to interact with them, is the commitment scale. This is especially the case if you have some stakeholders that aren't as supportive of your effort as you would like.

Understanding the project history so that you don't inadvertently repeat work that's already been done or rehash previously made decisions.

It's a common maxim (often attributed to George Santayana) that "those who do not learn history are doomed to repeat it."

When you work on an initiative that is entirely new—or at the least new to you—you don't want to repeat discussions that have already occurred, work that's already been done, or decisions that have already been made.

Teams working in an agile fashion get the reputation for not using documentation of any sort. The absolute view of no documentation is a myth, but it is quite common for initiatives to lack any real, useful institutional memory. Ironically, that happens just as frequently on phase-based efforts that produce tons of documentation but none that really helps you figure out what happened on the project in the past.

That said, if people working on the effort followed the premise of documentation with a purpose, there should be some system documentation that sheds light on the current state of the product.

If not, conversations with the stakeholders over coffee can be very helpful and often prove to be a very useful source of information about the initiative's history.

You certainly want to know what decisions have already been made and the resulting constraints so you know what boundaries you have to work within.

Techniques such as the purpose based alignment model and decision filters will help you establish a clear understanding of those constraints, and identify decisions already made that can guide future decisions for your product.

Understanding the existing systems and business processes so you have a reasonably clear picture of the current state that needs to change.

To get a clear picture of the context in which you're working, it's also important to learn about the other products, systems, organizations, and processes you'll interact with.

This is one of those places where your analysis skills are extremely relevant, with a slight change to the level and extent to which you use them.

Two techniques that are particularly useful are the context diagram—which helps you understand the different people, organizations, and systems your product interacts with—and process models—which help you get a better understanding of the process you'll support. In both cases, these techniques can help you build a strong understanding of the current context as well as what changes you'll make to the environment going forward.

For more information about the techniques mentioned above see:

- the User Modeling Technique Brief on KBP.media[93]
- the Personas Technique Brief on KBP.media[94]
- the Stakeholder Map Technique Brief on KBP.media[95]
- the Commitment Scale Technique Brief on KBP.media[96]
- the System Documentation Technique Brief on KBP.media[97]
- the Context Diagram Technique Brief on KBP.media[98]
- the Process Models Technique Brief on KBP.media[99]

Step 2 – Discover the primary business objective

You've probably been in this situation before. You start work on a new product, or want to change an existing internal product. It's an exciting time, there's work to be done. You can really make a difference.

You're tempted to pull everyone together into a room and start putting up sticky notes with all the great things you could do ...

I think perhaps you've forgotten something.

- Why are you building or changing that product?
- Do you know what problem you're trying to solve?
- How do you know if you're heading in the right direction?
- How will you know when you're successful?
- Do you know your *why*?

---

[93] https://www.kbp.media/user-modeling/
[94] https://www.kbp.media/personas/
[95] https://www.kbp.media/stakeholder-map/
[96] https://www.kbp.media/commitment-scale/
[97] https://www.kbp.media/system-documentation/
[98] https://www.kbp.media/context-diagram/
[99] https://www.kbp.media/process-model/

Unfortunately this is all too common. You have the irresistible urge to jump right into defining what you need to do—identifying your outputs—without first clearly understanding why you're doing something—understanding your desired outcome.

If you determine your outcome first and express that in a measurable fashion, you can use that as a decision filter to focus on the things that absolutely have to be done and avoid those things that don't contribute to what you're really trying to accomplish.

Do you have to wait until you fully understand your context before you identify the desired outcome? Not necessarily. You do need to identify the customers you are trying to serve first in order to understand the problem you're trying to solve, but you need to know the problem you're trying to solve in order to know what stakeholders may be involved.

This is just as important in an internal situation as it is in an external situation—perhaps even more important.

Key responsibilities

Discovering expectations from your primary stakeholders—essentially discovering the "why" behind the project.

When you work on an internal product, you need to decide what to do based on its impact to your customers, but you also need to consider your stakeholders. Chances are, those stakeholders are the users of the internal product, or have the users working for them. As a result, they will be very interested in what you're up to. It can be easy for those stakeholders to be more concerned about their own needs than your actual customers' needs.

Some ways that you can start work on an internal product include:

- Establishing a relationship with the sponsor (the business leader who wants to make sure the problem is solved).
- Discovering the desired outcomes.
- Establishing decision-making guardrails.
- Building a shared understanding with your team.

There are three techniques I've found particularly helpful for discovering the "why" for your effort. In all three cases, these techniques are ways to structure a conversation between the key players in your effort in order to identify the true why behind your effort.

The internal product opportunity assessment is a set of 10 questions to help lead your team, including your key stakeholders, through a discussion that identifies why you want to do something and whether it's worth it.

The problem statement may form an answer to one of the questions in the opportunity assessment, or it can act as a shorter version of that exercise. This technique helps you identify people's current view of why you're taking on a specific initiative and then provides a way of reaching a shared understanding.

Creating a project charter with your team and stakeholders can be a great way to discuss all the key points and come to a shared understanding of why you're pursuing the effort. There are several different formats that teams have found useful. All of those different approaches have the following characteristics in common:

- Your output is concise, usually about a page long.
- Your team has a shared understanding of the problem you're trying to solve.
- Your team has a shared understanding of how you'll know when you've solved that problem.
- You've identified any constraints which will impact the solution.

Reconciling conflicting expectations so that the business community begins the project with a shared understanding of the business objectives and are not restricted to one person's perspective.

Successful projects begin with a shared understanding of their business objectives—one that's not unique to one person's perspective. You satisfy this key responsibility by holding collaborative discussions with your team and stakeholders, so no additional techniques are needed.

You could head off-site, hole yourself up in some cabin in the woods, or write out a problem statement and then ask everyone on your team to read it and live it.

The problem with that approach is that your team and stakeholders do not get an opportunity to internalize what the project is about and clarify their viewpoints. If they rely on reading the description of the product, they will either interpret what they read to match their preconceived notions or they won't bother to read the document at all.

Ensuring the business objectives are clear and actionable to provide the project team with momentum and context while defining scope and, later on, the detailed requirements.

In order to truly know when you've delivered the outcome that you sought to deliver or solved the problem you set out to solve, you need some form of outcome based metrics. These are measurements that tell you quantitatively that you have helped your organization achieve some form of outcome, not merely delivered a specific output.

When defining outcome based metrics, I've found the characteristics of good objectives that Tom Gilb suggested in *Competitive Engineering* to be particularly helpful. I discussed these characteristics in Chapter 8.

The discussion that occurs in order to decide what the target and constraint should be allows the team to get a clearer understanding of what success looks like.

Understanding the desired outcome in terms of outcome based metrics gives you the opportunity to build a shared understanding with your team about why you are considering starting (or continuing) a particular project. It also gives you a basis for asking whether the need is worth satisfying.

For more information about the techniques mentioned above see:

- the Internal Product Opportunity Assessment Technique Brief on KBP.media[100]
- the Outcome Based Metric Technique Brief on KBP.media[101]

Step 3 – Define scope

Once you're oriented to the context in which you're working and you've established a shared understanding of the outcome you seek, it's time to identify the scope of your work.

When you're working in a situation with a great deal of certainty (you have a clear understanding of what needs to be done in order to accomplish the desired outcome) you can represent your scope as the collection of backlog items. Sort of.

You see, backlog items are *options*.

Just because an item shows up on the backlog does not mean it has to be done. Your gauge of whether something has to be done is the impact on your desired outcome.

In some cases, almost all the items you put on your backlog need to be done. This is often the case in initiatives with a lot of

---

[100] https://www.kbp.media/internal-product-opportunity-assessment/
[101] https://www.kbp.media/outcome-based-metrics/

certainty—where you're replacing an existing system, for example. In many cases, however, there is a great deal of uncertainty regarding the best way to accomplish something. In those cases, backlog items take on the role of options. You can't know the best approach at the beginning of the effort, so you put items on your backlog that will help you determine the best approach. As you deliver some work and see the impact on your desired outcome you'll build a better understanding of what you need to do and the number of necessary items on your backlog will grow.

The key is to not use scope, defined as a list of backlog items, as the ultimate measure of success. That should be the outcome based metric you already identified. Your backlog can still serve as "our current understanding of scope" with the realization that your understanding will change as you proceed. This is one of the key ideas behind design thinking: understand that there may be multiple ways to solve the problem and experiment with different solutions to find the one that works best.

Key responsibilities

Defining a solution approach to determine the nature and extent of technology and business process changes to be made as part of implementing the solution to the primary business objectives.

When you're in a fairly certain environment, you can identify a solution and then populate a product backlog from that view of the solution. If you're doing work to support a business process, you may find it helpful to create a process model and use that to identify backlog items. You may also find a story map helpful to understand the entire process you're trying to support and to identify potential ways to support that process.

When you have an outcome identified but are not sure of the best way to get there, an impact map can be extremely helpful. You start with your outcome, identify the people who can help you reach that outcome or prevent you from reaching that outcome, determine the behaviors that will drive those impacts, and then determine the deliverables that you can deliver to help change those behaviors. After each deliverable you deliver, you check the impact on the objective and then decide whether you are done or if you need to try another deliverable.

These deliverables are the input to your product backlog, but you only want to have the deliverable you are currently working on in the backlog.

Keep in mind that you'll more than likely have more items in your backlog than you're going to deliver. The backlog represents things you could do, not things you absolutely have to do. The backlog also represents your understanding of scope at the moment, not the final definition of scope.

Drafting a scope statement and reviewing it with your key business and technology stakeholders until they are prepared to sign off or buy in to the document.

When you work in an agile fashion, your agreement with and commitment to your stakeholders is not based on scope, but rather on reaching a specific outcome. You don't have a scope statement that addresses your agreement. You agree on the outcome you seek to deliver (described using an outcome based metric) and then you establish a backlog with potential ways to achieve that outcome. You review your progress on a regular basis with your stakeholders and confirm whether the backlog includes the appropriate items in the appropriate order.

There is no single sign-off. Rather, there are a series of agreements to proceed for the next couple of weeks based on what everyone understands at the time.

If you're using sprints, sprint reviews are a good time to recheck those agreements. If you're working in a flow approach, you may check progress after every item is completed or on a regular cadence once every week or two.

Confirming the business case to ensure that it still makes sense for your organization to invest in the project.

A part of those ongoing discussions and agreements is a discussion about whether the problem is still worth addressing at all, and whether it's worth it to address the problem with the chosen solution.

As you deliver new outputs and check the impact on the outcome, you're learning more about the problem and possible solution(s). You may learn something which indicates that it's going to cost more to solve the problem than the problem is costing.

Or, you may find out you can use a different solution to address the problem for less.

Step 4 – Formulate your business analysis plan

Perhaps the biggest difference between business analysts in a phase-based, "waterfall" approach and an iterative "agile" approach is when you do a majority of your work. In most phased-based approaches you perform all of your analysis at the beginning of the project in order to create a (sometimes quite substantial) requirements document.

In an iterative approach, that aspect of analysis gets spread throughout the entire initiative. You do a little bit of work to establish the breadth of your initiative at the beginning, but you stay at a fairly high level. Then, as your team starts to deliver small increments of the solution you do a deep dive into each subset of the solution as needed. Commonly, you're doing a deep dive on the backlog items your team will most likely deliver next while they're working on backlog items that they plan to deliver now.

This change in when you do analysis means that you need to dramatically reconsider what you think of when you hear "business analysis plan."

The business analysis plan was always about setting expectations with your team regarding the output of your analysis efforts, but most people looked to the plan as a list of people to talk to and documents to produce.

When you work in an agile fashion, it's helpful to focus on the expectation-setting aspect of the business analysis plan. In effect, you're forming an agreement—dare I say, a shared understanding—about what information, and what format, you and your team will use to build a shared understanding about the solution you're going to deliver.

The techniques I've found most helpful to build and maintain that shared understanding are the discovery board and the Definition of ready, along with a healthy dose of refining that understanding during retrospectives and general discussions among the team.

You and your team may also establish some agreements about what system documentation you want to create and maintain while you're building the solution so you have reference information for future efforts.

You'll see more about how to use those techniques in the discussion of the key responsibilities below.

Key responsibilities

Choosing the most appropriate types of business analysis deliverables, given the project scope, project methodology, and other key aspects of the project context.

You want to reach an agreement with your team about what information they would find helpful to start developing a part of the solution represented by a backlog item. You also want to come to agreement on the best format for conveying that information.

I hesitate to call those items "business analysis deliverables" because they really belong to the entire team, but chances are the things that get produced (jointly by you and the rest of your team) are going to look awfully familiar. As you'll see in the next step, the techniques you use to describe backlog items are often some of the more frequently used business analysis techniques.

In order to come to an agreement about how your team will communicate and remember the specifics about the solution and individual backlog items, it's helpful to create a Definition of ready. The Definition of ready indicates the information that your team would like to have in place to consider a backlog item for inclusion in a sprint. It's how you know the backlog item is "ready" for development work to begin. It's also a good indicator as to when you've done enough analysis on that backlog item.

You jointly create the Definition of ready with your team, and you revise that definition based on your team's experience of delivering backlog items and your experience of guiding the effort to get those backlog items ready.

Defining the specific list of business analysis deliverables that will completely cover the scope of the project and identifying the stakeholders who will be part of the creation and validation of each deliverable.

As part of your plan, you need to define the specific list of business analysis deliverables that will completely cover the scope of the project and identify the stakeholders who will help create and validate each deliverable. There's a great deal of overlap between this key responsibility and the previous one, especially when your perspective on requirements changes from an end in and of themselves to a means to an end.

Additionally, this responsibility drives the system documentation your team needs to maintain. System documentation is that reference information you want to keep around after you've delivered your product so you have something to refer to when you need to make changes in the future.

The items usually identified in the Definition of ready are "project documentation" that notes the changes from the current state of the product to the desired new state. Those items usually aren't organized in a very helpful manner for reference or ongoing maintenance. That's where system documentation comes in handy. It's built to be easy to reference and easy to maintain. There's no need to duplicate information that can be derived directly from the product itself. The system documentation should provide supplementary information not immediately apparent in the product.

Another aspect of this responsibility is identifying the key stakeholders you need to interact with in order to successfully deliver the product. A stakeholder map can serve as a guide for determining how to interact with those stakeholders, but you still need to actually interact with them.

Identifying the timelines for completing the business analysis deliverables.

Due to the switch from creating a set of deliverables at the beginning of a project to fleshing out the specifics of certain work items on a regular basis, the concept of timelines and deadlines takes on a different meaning. Instead of having one significant timeline, you have repeating targets for getting product backlog items ready, which usually correlates to right before sprint planning.

I've found the discovery board helpful in making the progress of backlog items more transparent. You won't necessarily have a series of timelines so much as a visual display of where items are and whether you'll have enough to fill up your team's capacity.

Step 5 – Define the detailed requirements

You've determined the overall scope for your initiative and created a broad understanding of your solution. Now it's time to deliver an increment of that solution—something minimal enough that you can get fast feedback, but substantial enough that the solution is viable enough for that feedback to be meaningful.

In order to deliver part of a solution that's minimal and viable, you need to make sure your team has a shared understanding of the problem and solution.

When you're ready to start delivering increments of your solution, select an item (or collection of items) from your backlog and delve into more detail about it. Backlog items are generally recorded in the form of user stories, so I'll refer to them as such.

Don't get sucked into all the chatter about how important it is to write user stories in the proper fashion. It is important to make sure a user story represents something that helps you ultimately achieve the outcome you seek. Beyond that, how you write it is not as important as you might think. That's because user stories were never intended to be the sole means of describing the solution, and they were certainly not intended to be the only means by which you build shared understanding. They are placeholders for the conversations you have in order to build that shared understanding. You also shouldn't take that to mean that you don't record any information about the solution at all.

In other words, we don't rely on user stories themselves to describe what we're building. They're the outline. The description comes in the form of the models, acceptance criteria, and examples we create during our conversations and keep around as we build the product.

Start with a user story that you think your team will want to deliver soon—within the next sprint if you're using Scrum, for example. Determine if there are any key stakeholders you need to talk to in order to understand the intent of the user story. Invite a couple members of your team that can look at the situation from the perspective of development (what could we build to solve the problem the user story represents) and testing (what happens when). You may also want to include someone who has insight into good user experience. Have a conversation with that small group to get a better understanding of the user story. Those conversations are what many teams refer to as backlog refinement.

Talk through what the user story is trying to accomplish. As you talk, create one or more models to aid your conversation. The model you pick varies depending on the type of problem you're trying to solve:

- If you're providing support for a business process, a process model is probably best.
- If you're solving a problem that involves collecting a lot of information, a user interface is going to be your best bet.
- If you're solving a problem by presenting a lot of information, you'll want to mockup a report.

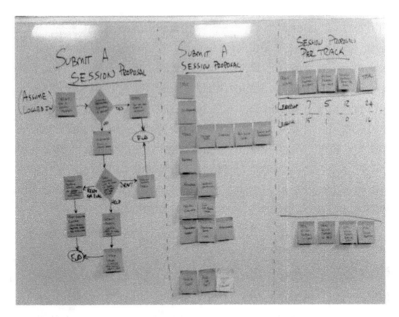

Figure 24. Drafting a model of your solution, like this process model for a conference submission system, helps the team build shared understanding of the backlog items needed to address a user story.

You may choose to structure your conversation using example mapping; this can help you identify acceptance criteria and examples that you can use to further describe the user story and build that shared understanding with your team.

The model provides the rich information about the user story that pictures always provide. The acceptance criteria fill in the gaps that the picture can't convey and provide further understanding of how you know when you've delivered the user story successfully. Examples help clarify your expectations about how the solution behaves in certain circumstances.

You may craft some of this information before you chat with your stakeholders and team members so that they have something to react to, rather than starting with a clean slate. You may have conversations with your stakeholders first, and then discuss what you found out with your team. Your approach depends on how your team chooses to operate.

Just remember that the more separate conversations you have, the longer it will take to get to a shared understanding. Consider the trade-offs involved with your selected approach.

Remember that the goal is not to create requirements. The goal is to build a shared understanding of the problem you're trying to solve and your desired solution. Requirements are a tool you can use to build that shared understanding.

Key responsibilities

The key responsibilities described below sound as though there are three distinct activities that occur when you build detailed understanding. If you're facilitating the conversations described above correctly, you actually fulfill all three responsibilities at the same time.

Eliciting the information necessary to understand what the business community wants from a specific feature or process change.

As you talk with your stakeholders and team about the user story, you want to understand the intent of the backlog item and how it supports achieving the overall outcome.

As you discuss the user story, you may identify questions that require follow up. To keep those conversations productive, it's helpful to note those questions and agree to research outside the conversation and follow up with everyone, rather than continuing the conversation in a swirl around that particular question when you don't stand a chance of uncovering any new information.

If you use example mapping to structure those conversations, you have a built-in way of identifying questions for further follow up: red index cards.

Analyzing the information you've discovered and using it to create a first draft of one or more business analysis deliverables containing the detailed requirements for the project.

Shared understanding is more important than any artifacts you put together to build (or remember) that shared understanding. That said, those artifacts are first drafts of what you could call *business analysis deliverables*. The models, acceptance criteria, and examples you identify during the conversations to describe the user story can also help you remember what you talked about.

You may expand on those artifacts if the team feels like they need more information to accurately describe the desired solution. This most often happens when you identify relevant examples in conversations with your stakeholders, and then flesh out those examples with gherkin (given-when-then) afterward so that your team has specifics to refer to.

Reviewing and validating each deliverable with appropriate business and technology stakeholders and asking questions to fill in any gaps.

When you discuss the backlog item with your stakeholders and team, you simultaneously uncover the intent, discuss the specifics, and validate that everyone has the same understanding of the user story.

If your team chose to have you sketch some specifics out ahead of time and then discuss it with them, those discussions take on a bit more of a review and validation nature.

Either way, the intent is not to determine whether the "requirements are correct." Rather, it's to confirm that the stakeholders and team have the same understanding of the intent and specifics of the user story. That is a subtle but important difference.

Step 6 – Support the technical implementation

No matter how diligent you are, no matter how many times you discuss things, no matter how many process models you sketch, acceptance criteria you define, or examples you identify, your team is going to still have questions.

Just accept it.

When there are questions, that doesn't necessarily mean you did a bad job describing the backlog item. You're running into a reality of knowledge work in general and software development in particular: you learn throughout the entire process.

What all this means is that you will spend part of your time working with the team as they build the solution and part of your time getting the next backlog items ready.

There are certainly advantages to spending time with your team as they build the solution. You can get an idea of what questions come up as they dig into a backlog item, which may help you to revise your approach to getting the next items ready.

It's not bad when your team has questions about a backlog item you've already described. It is bad if your team has the same question about one backlog item after another. That's a sign that you aren't learning from experience.

Key responsibilities

Reviewing the solution design to ensure it fulfills all of the requirements and looking for opportunities to meet additional business needs without increasing the technical scope of the project.

The solution design should fulfill all of the requirements. As you review for that, look for opportunities to meet additional business needs without increasing the technical scope of the project.

This type of review primarily occurs when you get your backlog items ready, so the applicable part of this responsibility is dealing with additional business needs that your team identifies while building the solution, or that your stakeholders realize they hadn't identified yet.

When new business needs come up, it's tempting to point accusingly at whoever brings up the new need and shout "Scope Creep" at the top of your lungs.

Whether that's an accurate assessment depends on how you define *scope*. If you define scope based solely on output (the backlog items you deliver) then it sure feels like additional scope. If instead you define scope based on the outcome, the label *scope creep* is unfair. It's merely a clarification of understanding.

Here's how these new needs usually come up: Your team starts working on a backlog item, and as they build the solution someone asks "What happens in this situation?" You'd like to get most of these questions identified during example mapping, but some will inevitably sneak through.

Your role when this occurs is to talk through the situation with your team. Make sure they have a shared understanding of the need. I've come across many situations where a new business need some people thought they found was really just a misunderstanding.

Try to understand how frequently the new situation occurs (or whether it's actually real). Identify existing aspects of the solution that may address the need and then figure out a way to address the need with as little work as possible.

Updating and/or repackaging requirements documentation to make it useful for the technology design and implementation process.

Remember that requirements are a means to an end. The purpose of analysis activities is building a shared understanding, not creating requirements.

With that in mind, if you find that the way you describe backlog items could use some improvement, you'll most likely adjust your approach describing future backlog items rather than by dramatically changing how you've described the current backlog items. Sure, you may update the information you recorded about the current item to reflect anything the team discovered in order to maintain a shared understanding, but you probably won't make substantial changes to an item that will be delivered within the next week.

Resist the urge to update backlog items merely to reflect how they ended up getting implemented for future reference. That's the purpose of system documentation, which will generally be a different artifact created specifically to provide information for your product as built. Backlog items are intended to be temporary artifacts that describe the change needed to go from current state to future state.

Engaging with quality assurance professionals to ensure they understand the business context for the technical requirements. This responsibility may include reviewing test plans and/or test cases to ensure they represent a clear understanding of the functional requirements.

This responsibility should probably be included in Step 5. You want to include people with a quality assurance outlook in your backlog refinement discussions so they can suggest what-if scenarios and learn the business context through involvement in those discussions.

If QA people don't get up to speed on backlog items until those items are being built, you run the risk of not having a shared understanding. You also introduce the likelihood of delays delivering those backlog items, because your QA people may not be ready to validate the solution when the team finishes developing it. Finally, you'll end up with different views of acceptance criteria because the people who implemented the backlog item don't have the same understanding of success as the people who are validating it.

Making yourself available to answer questions and help resolve any issues that surface during the technical design, technical implementation, or testing phases of the project.

The spirit of this responsibility is right on, although it should probably be reworded as "Make yourself available to answer questions and help resolve any issues that surface as backlog items are developed and tested."

You don't have technical design, technical implementation, or testing phases. Those activities happen on an ongoing basis, as does a deeper understanding of backlog items (see Step 5).

Managing requirements changes to ensure that everyone is working from up-to-date documentation and that appropriate stakeholders are involved in all decisions about change.

Not only do you build shared understanding, but you also need to maintain it throughout the initiative. As your team identifies new scenarios for a specific backlog item or new needs, work with the team and stakeholders to make sure everyone is aware of the new information and discuss an appropriate way to address that new information.

When appropriate, leading user acceptance testing efforts completed by the business community to ensure that the software implementation meets the needs of business end users.

Whenever you can, give your users an opportunity to have meaningful exposure to your product as soon as possible so that they can use it and provide meaningful feedback.

You may need to change your view of acceptance testing from "test to make sure we delivered the solution correctly" to "determine whether this solution solves our problem." This change in perspective means that you no longer ask your users to duplicate testing your team is most likely (or should be) doing, and instead focus on whether the solution solves their problem.

Your role in this is to help your users understand the purpose of doing that acceptance testing, and to help them structure their testing efforts so that they can achieve that purpose.

User acceptance testing is also a great way to help with the next step by getting your users familiar with the solution.

Step 7 – Help the business implement the solution

It's always been important for your users to understand and properly use the new features you deliver.

You'll have much more interest in helping them use new features properly when you define success based on achieving a specific outcome, instead of merely delivering the features your team said they would deliver.

You may think that this is all about training users on new features, and that's certainly part of this step. It's also important to think about what other changes (such as business processes, work instructions, and policies) need to occur to get to your desired outcome.

You'll also want to consider what transition activities result from the changes your team made, such as updating data to work appropriately with the new functionality your team built.

It's best to consider the activities in this step early—such as when you identify potential solutions. You may discover that it's possible to achieve your desired outcome with process and policy changes, and without any software changes.

Understanding what you need to do to implement the solution can also help define what transition activities are required so you can plan for the time necessary to do those activities, and perhaps incorporate some of those transition needs into the team's work.

Training users is also important. That training should cover not only the changes to your product itself, but also the business processes impacted by your product or the changes to it. You can forgo training, but only if you build your product to be so intuitive that training on the software itself is not necessary. I realize that is easier said than done. (I can attest to that from personal experience.)

If the nature of your product is such that you still need to provide some training to users, you don't have to wait until you're delivering the product to show them how to use it. Use reviews to not only show customers, users, and stakeholders what your team is working on and get feedback, but also to show how the product works. Let them try it out.

As with the previous two steps, this is not a one-time occurrence. It happens every time you deliver a new increment of the solution to your users. The good news is, since you (hopefully) deliver small aspects of the solution, you can focus on a small set of changes.

Ironically, the frequency of your deliveries may be driven by whether your stakeholders are able, or willing, to make small, frequent changes to their processes.

Key responsibilities

Analyzing and developing interim and future state business process documentation that articulates exactly what changes need to be made to the business process.

The extent to which you carry out this responsibility is based on the extent of your process documentation. As with all documentation, it's best to create documentation with a purpose.

Complete enough documentation to properly convey the necessary information, but make it no more complex or extensive than necessary. It doesn't have to be extravagant. As with the features, any documentation you provide or update related to business process changes should focus on building and maintaining shared understanding and should not be considered the sole means of communicating business process changes.

This is often an activity that's best performed collaboratively with your stakeholders and users. If you work together to discuss and revise impacted business processes, your stakeholders and users are going to have a better understanding of the changes, and they will bring their knowledge and understanding to bear to make sure you consider all of the necessary changes.

Training end users to ensure they understand all process and procedural changes or collaborating with training staff so they can create appropriate training materials and deliver the training.

Sometimes a general overview of the changes that you're making is sufficient. In other cases you may need to put together reference material for users, and in others you may need training sessions to get your users up to speed.

The more intuitive you make your product, the more likely you only have to provide specifics of upcoming changes and possibly user documentation.

Once you've provided user guides, your ongoing changes should not require completely new guides as much as updates to the existing guides.

A word of warning: it can be very easy to forget to change your existing user guide, so be sure to incorporate some mechanism to remember to update that documentation when you make changes.

An example of a user guide is the Submission System Guide[102] I put together for Agile Alliance's Submission System.

Collaborating with business users to update other organizational assets impacted by the business process and technology changes.

Most of the work you do with your stakeholders and users to roll out changes helps them revise impacted business processes and get up to speed on changes to your product. There will always be other items you need to update. Those items may include:

- Work instructions for people who may not use your product but may be impacted by it.
- Communication to customers about how the changes you've made will impact them.
- Communications to stakeholders outside your organization that may be impacted by the changes you made. Depending on the impact, this communication should happen before you deliver the changes.

An organizational asset that you'll need to update, and which is often forgotten until deployment, is any data that the process uses or product processes. When you start working on changes, think about the data involved and how it's impacted:

---

[102] https://www.agilealliance.org/submission-system-guide

- Do you need to transform any data when you implement your changes?
- Do you need to update other systems that use data from your product?
- Are there reports that need to be updated or created?
- Are there provisions you need to make to track metrics that you identified as measures of success?

Remember, no matter how effectively you communicate with your stakeholders, users, or customers they will still have questions when you implement your solution. When those questions come up, don't look on it as a failure in your communication. See those questions as an opportunity to identify how to improve communication for the next roll out. Chances are you'll have plenty of opportunities.

Step 8 – Assess value created by the solution

Assessing value created by the solution is critical to the effectiveness of an iterative, outcome- focused approach and ultimately to the effectiveness of your organization. This step is relevant for all efforts, but it becomes even more important when you follow an iterative, outcome- focused approach. Instead of something that just happens once at the end of a project, this is something that should occur every time you deliver changes so you can determine whether you should keep going, change your course, or stop the initiative. Unfortunately, it's a step that is not practiced not nearly as often as it should be.

This step is tied closely with Step 2 - Discover the primary business objectives. That step identifies the metric you'll want to use measure success. Step 8 encourages the use of that metric to determine if your work is moving in the right direction.

Assessing value is not a one-time thing. You want to measure the impact of your most recent change to determine if you've solved the problem and identify your next steps. If you've reached your target, that's a sign that you can stop work on this initiative and try to solve a different problem. If the metric is moving in the wrong direction, your team can determine whether you should back out the changes you just made, because you may have made the situation worse. If you're making some progress but still aren't happy, you can continue to work on the current problem and make further changes.

It comes down to using an agreed-upon indicator relevant to your organization to determine success, rather than gauging success based on deploying a specific set of outputs.

Key responsibilities

Evaluating the actual progress made against the business objectives for the project to show the extent to which the original objectives have been fulfilled.

One of the most meaningful ways you can help your team focus on outcome over output is to check the metric you're targeting every time you deliver a change to your users. You want to see if the change you made is moving you closer to your target.

Depending on your metric, you may need to allow a certain amount of time for the changes to your product and process to take effect. For example, if the metric you're looking at is a monthly measure, you'll need to wait at least a month before checking the metric and assessing the effectiveness of the change.

As a result, it helps to select metrics that have a shorter timeframe so you can shorten the feedback cycle. Instead of a monthly metric, look for metrics that you can explore weekly.

Communicating the results to the project sponsor, and if appropriate, to the project team and all members of the organization.

I'd change the text of this responsibility to remove "and if appropriate." Your team needs to be up to speed on the impact your changes have on your target metric. You want them to make the appropriate day-to-day decisions to accomplish the desired outcome.

You also need to create a mechanism to keep people informed of your objective and your current progress toward that objective.

Conveying the status of your business objective is not a one-time communication. It's an ongoing communication that you update after you introduce changes to your product or the corresponding processes.

Suggesting follow-up projects and initiatives to fully realize the intended business objectives of the project or to solve new problems that are discovered while evaluating the impact of this project.

When your team follows an iterative, incremental, and outcome-focused approach you examine your business objective after every change. So you're not suggesting follow-up projects and initiatives, you're suggesting whether to continue to try to solve the current problem or move on to something else.

If your team follows this approach appropriately, you get away from the all-too-common situation where your stakeholders expect you to cram everything they asked for in the first delivery because they're not certain they are going to get any follow-up attention.

Deliver a small increment that you think might solve the problem you face, deliver it early, check on the result. If you didn't meet your target, you should still have some time and budget left to try something else.

This responsibility is about answering the question "Are we done?" in an outcome based way.